STRUCTURED ON-THE-JOB TRAINING

STRUCTURED ON-THE-JOB TRAINING

Unleashing Employee Expertise in the Workplace

SECOND EDITION

Ronald L. Jacobs

BK·

BERRETT-KOEHLER PUBLISHERS, INC.
San Francisco

Berrett-Koehler Publishers, Inc.
235 Montgomery, Suite 650
San Francisco, CA 94104-2916
Tel: (415) 288-0260   Fax: (415) 362-2512   www.bkconnection.com

ORDERING INFORMATION

Quantity sales. Special discounts are available on quantity purchases by corporations, associations, and others. For details, contact the "Special Sales Department" at the Berrett-Koehler address above.

Individual sales. Berrett-Koehler publications are available through most bookstores. They can also be ordered direct from Berrett-Koehler: Tel: (800) 929-2929; Fax: (802) 864-7626; www.bkconnection.com

Orders for college textbook/course adoption use. Please contact Berrett-Koehler: Tel: (800) 929-2929; Fax: (802) 864-7626.

Orders by U.S. trade bookstores and wholesalers. Please contact Publishers Group West, 1700 Fourth Street, Berkeley, CA 94710. Tel: (510) 528-1444; Fax (510) 528-3444.

Production Management: Michael Bass & Associates

Berrett-Koehler and the BK logo are registered trademarks of Berrett-Koehler Publishers, Inc.

Printed in the United States of America

Berrett-Koehler books are printed on long-lasting acid-free paper. When it is available, we choose paper that has been manufactured by environmentally responsible processes. These may include using trees grown in sustainable forests, incorporating recycled paper, minimizing chlorine in bleaching, or recycling the energy produced at the paper mill.

Library of Congress Cataloging-in-Publication Data

Jacobs, Ronald L.
   Structured on-the-job training: unleashing employee expertise in the workplace / Ronald L. Jacobs.—2nd ed.
     p. cm.
   Includes bibliographical references and index.
   ISBN 1-57675-242-9
   1. Employees—Training of. 2. Employees—Training of—Evaluation
I. Title.
   HF5549.5.T7 J25 2002
   658.3'1243—dc21

                                2002034506

Second Edition
08 07 06 05 04 03   10 9 8 7 6 5 4 3 2 1

One must learn by doing the thing; for though you think you know it, you have no certainty until you try.

—SOPHOCLES, 496–406 BC *(Chorus, Trachiniae)*

Contents

Preface

This second edition has a decidedly different emphasis from the first edition. The first edition of this book essentially introduced the point that on-the-job training (OJT) in organizations could be structured, or planned, in nature and that it could result in more reliable and predictable training outcomes. Making such an assertion seemed appropriate at that time, given that relatively few organization managers or human resource development (HRD) professionals had considered OJT in this way. Indeed, experience showed that most people in organizations continued to view OJT as being mostly unstructured. Thus, the first edition of the book, in large part, took on the mission of promoting the use of structured on-the-job training, or S-OJT™, as a training approach.

The goal of the second edition is to expand and extend the initial emphasis, but without losing the fundamental message. Introducing a second edition suggests that it is sufficiently different to make the investment worthwhile to the reader. The second edition has much new information blended into existing chapters and has added four new chapters, indicating that the past several years have been extremely fruitful ones for advancing the theory, research, and practice related to S-OJT. Many more practitioners and scholars have begun to focus their professional energies in this direction. And more resources are now available on the topic than ever before. From a few voices heard on the topic just a few years ago, a group of like-minded individuals has emerged. Indeed, entering *structured on-the-job training* on any Web search engine brings forward a wide range of links in which the term appears.

Some have asked what more could be said about S-OJT? There is apparently much more to be said, and there seems no end in sight, given our era of rapid change. Of course, all of this interest is good in the long run for improving HRD practice and, by extension, for improving organizations and society in general.

This broader perspective represents the second edition. That is, the book seeks to address how S-OJT can help respond to the ever-changing competence needs of individuals already employed in organizations and those preparing to be employed in the future. In truth, S-OJT practices have moved in directions that could not have been predicted just a few years ago—such as being used with high school youth entering work-based training programs and being part of publicly funded economic development efforts. Indeed, while the first edition made important advances at the time, it looks inadequate in some respects when viewed in today's more global economic context. Thus, the time seemed appropriate to introduce this second edition.

As stated, the fundamental issue being addressed is how people learn to do their work. Almost all employees have experienced some form of OJT in their working life, regardless of job level or type of organization. Few, if any, training programs in a setting away from their work can present all areas of knowledge and skill effectively. In a practical sense, OJT helps employees bridge the gap between learning and making use of what was learned. And OJT offers the potential benefit that some useful work might even be accomplished during the training period.

While some time has passed since publication, the estimates by Carnevale and Gainer (1989) continue to seem appropriate for consideration:

- Eighty to 90 percent of an employee's job and knowledge will probably be learned through OJT.

- Organizations will spend three times more per employee for OJT than for off-the-job training, even if there is no designated budget item for OJT.

- Up to one-third of an employee's first-year salary is devoted to OJT costs.

Unfortunately, most OJT in organizations continues to be unplanned and thus potentially harmful to organizations and individuals. Expediency is often the major reason for using unstructured OJT, and the likely consequences of its use are often not considered. In the eyes of many managers, OJT has few or no costs and can be implemented quickly and easily. The training process is often left to other employees who, while they may know their jobs, are relatively unskilled as trainers. Such an approach is often the major argument made against the use of OJT. As a result, many organizations rely on off-the-job training without considering its suitability for the learning task at hand.

An increasing number of managers and HRD professionals appreciate two basic truths about the training that occurs in their organizations. First:

Training programs have a strategic role in organizations.

The global economy, which demands increased flexibility in production and service delivery, use of advanced technologies, and increased responsiveness to customers' needs, continues to emphasize the strategic importance of high levels of employee know-how or expertise. High-performing and successful organizations depend on employees who can effectively solve problems and make decisions. But as tasks have become increasingly complex, they have also been subject to constant change. Second:

OJT does not have to be ineffective.

As a result, *structured* on-the-job training has become part of the lexicon of the HRD field. The term *structured* simply means that the training has undergone adequate forethought and planning.

These two basic truths have done much to promote the present level of interest in S-OJT as a training approach. While S-OJT has many features in common with other forms of structured training, it is distinct in other respects. For example, it emphasizes one-on-one contact between experienced and novice employees as the primary means of conveying training content. By concentrating on S-OJT, this book addresses an important need in the literature on management and human resource development.

Specifically, this book provides a comprehensive guide to understand, develop, and use S-OJT. Its underlying goal is to improve the training approaches currently used to develop high levels of employee competence, or expertise, in the workplace. Once developed, this expertise can be unleashed or made available to help solve problems for the benefit of individuals, organizations, and societies alike. To achieve this goal, principles have been drawn from sound theory and proven professional practice. Useful theory comes from sound practice, and sound practice produces predictable and consistent results—the same ends that managers in organizations have for their business processes.

A system view of S-OJT remains the cornerstone of the book. A system view ensures that S-OJT is understood in the same way that organizations are understood. Both S-OJT and organizations must be considered as dynamic systems that have their own sets of inputs, processes, and outputs. System designers are often concerned with how systems work together, and the same concern applies to structured OJT. S-OJT as a training system comes into direct contact with another system, the work system. How organizations reconcile training and working when S-OJT is used is an issue of primary importance.

PLAN OF THE BOOK

The fifteen chapters of the book are grouped into three parts. Part One, "Meeting the Demand for Employee Expertise," provides a rationale for the use of S-OJT and a framework for understanding it. Chapter 1 introduces the notion of employee expertise and shows that the need for developing such expertise effectively and efficiently has prompted much of the recent interest in S-OJT. Chapter 2 defines the system view of S-OJT, discussing the features that make it different from other training approaches. Chapter 3 discusses S-OJT as a form of formal learning and compares it with informal learning on the job, a topic of growing interest.

Part Two describes the steps involved in developing S-OJT. Chapter 4 examines the ways of using S-OJT and shows how one decides whether to use S-OJT for a given unit of work. Chapter 5 discusses how to conduct a work analysis in the preparation of S-OJT modules. Chapter 6 covers the selection, training, and management of S-OJT trainers. Chapter 7 presents the preparation of S-OJT modules. Chapters 8 and 9 describe the delivery process. And Chapter 10 discusses the evaluation and troubleshooting of S-OJT programs. The chapters include checklists, summary lists, or examples to guide readers through the steps involved.

Part Three, "Using Structured OJT," addresses the implementation of S-OJT. Chapter 11 presents how S-OJT has been used as part of the organizational change process, especially in addressing the need for increased employee flexibility. Chapter 12 discusses cross-cultural issues and how S-OJT has been used in the global context. Chapter 13 describes how S-OJT is being used as part of workforce development, an area that will likely help define S-OJT in the future. Chapter 14 makes the point that S-OJT should be implemented within a change management process. It also examines the issues involved in its use. Finally, Chapter 15 calls for the development of an organizational culture of employee expertise based on the use of S-OJT and other training approaches that encourage continuous learning.

Finally, Appendix A presents an excerpted portion of the Training within Industry (TWI) Report (Dooley, 1945) describing the influential lens grinder study. The TWI program during World War II first established S-OJT as a reliable means to improve organizational performance. The appendices also include documents of interest to developing S-OJT programs.

ACKNOWLEDGMENTS

The second edition of this book benefited much from the continuing interest and support of numerous friends and colleagues throughout the globe, in both university and organizational settings. I especially wish to acknowledge Ohio State University for providing me the time to complete the second edition. Finally, I am thankful to Marsha Jenkins, my partner and wife, for her continued love and insight. To them all, I say thanks.

PART ONE
MEETING THE
DEMAND FOR
EMPLOYEE EXPERTISE

Part One argues that developing high levels of employee competence is one of the most challenging issues for organizations. The proved efficiency and effectiveness of structured on-the-job training makes it especially suitable for meeting this challenge. Most other forms of training that occur in the work setting are essentially unstructured in nature.

Chapter 1
The Challenge of Developing Employee Expertise

The primary goal of this book is to provide a practical guide to understanding, developing, and using S-OJT. It seems important first to examine why this training approach has attracted increasing interest among many managers and human resource development (HRD) professionals. Thus, while presenting the rationale for the book as a whole, this first chapter addresses:

- employee expertise and the situations that affect expertise in the global economy,
- how organizations develop employee expertise through training, and
- issues that have prompted the recent interest in S-OJT.

EXPERTISE IN THE GLOBAL ECONOMY

Most people have faced the challenge of learning new knowledge and skills as part of their job. Training programs are designed to make this learning easier and less threatening. Yet, training is not meant to benefit individual employees only. The organization expects benefits from employees' training. In fact, training helps ensure that employees can do what the organization asks of them. Thus, training is ultimately about the issue of developing high levels of employee competence, or expertise.

Expertise is what experts know and can do. *Experts* are the individuals who are the most capable in specific areas of human endeavor. History has seen a great variety of experts: nomadic hunters who fashioned hunting tools from pieces of flint; mathematicians who planned the Egyptian pyramids; Renaissance artists who represented three dimensions in their paintings; eighteenth-century craftsmen who manufactured precision machine tools; managers today who devise strategic plans to guide the future of their organizations. Without the expertise of skilled persons, it is unlikely that our civilization could have advanced in the way it has over the millennium.

While expertise has been important for human progress, it is particularly important in contemporary organizations. The global economy demands increased flexibility in production and service delivery, improved use of advanced technologies, and increased responsiveness to the requirements of customers, and these demands have made expertise more prized than ever before (Jacobs & Washington, 2002; Carnevale, 1991). Drawing on the results of a four-year study, Kotter and Heskett (1992) suggest that the competitiveness of many organizations is determined largely by the knowledge, skills, and attitudes of the people in them. Peter Drucker (1993) states that knowledge is the primary resource for organizations in the present postcapitalist society.

Organizations must transform themselves if they are to become more competitive, and the competence of individual employees has become critical for ensuring the success of the transformation process. More than ever before, high-performing and successful organizations depend on employees who can perform complex tasks, such as solving problems and making decisions. But employees can perform complex tasks only if they possess the necessary knowledge and skills. Thus, when individual employees possess higher levels of competence, the organization as a whole is more able to respond effectively to the challenges it may face.

The reality of contemporary organizations is that most employees are being asked to develop higher levels of competence rapidly and continuously without undue interference in the ongoing work of their organization. All too often, competence requirements shift just as employees have come to feel comfortable with current ways. Customer service representatives—a function that appears, in various forms, in organizations—have been especially prone to such sudden changes in their work requirements. And when a new inventory management system is installed, a large portion of the knowledge and skills associated with the old system is no longer required.

In contrast to an organization's other resources, such as cash and equipment, human competence is not concrete. One cannot see it or reach out and touch it. Nevertheless, managing competence is often more central to an organization than managing its tangible resources. At the same time, the effects of expertise are clearly observable. When employees use their abilities to perform work, their efforts produce a range of outcomes.

People who possess the highest levels of competence are called experts. By definition, experts achieve the most valuable outcomes in organizations. Being an expert is but one level of human competence. Table 1.1 shows human competence categorized into a taxonomy ranging from a novice to that of a master (Jacobs & Washington, 2003). People whose outcomes are less valuable or who produce no outcomes can have lower levels of competence. These individuals are novices, or beginners. Those individuals who can perform specific tasks and achieve a limited range of work outcomes in doing those tasks, can be considered as specialists. When those individuals have some experience with the tasks over

TABLE 1.1. Levels of Human Competence	
Category	*Description*
NOVICE	Literally, one who is new to a work situation. There is often some but minimal exposure to the work beforehand. As a result, the individual lacks the knowledge and skills necessary to meet the requirements set to adequately perform the work.
SPECIALIST	One who can reliably perform specific units of work unsupervised. But the range of work is limited to the most routine ones. Often it is necessary to coach individuals at this level to help them use the most appropriate behaviors.
EXPERIENCED SPECIALIST	One who can perform specific units of work and who has performed that work repeatedly. As a result, the individual can perform the work with ease and skill. It is possible to remain at this level for an extended period of time.
EXPERT	One who has the knowledge and experience to meet and often exceed the requirements of performing a particular unit of work. The individual is respected by others and highly regarded by peers because of his or her consummate skills, or expertise. The individual can use this ability to deal with routine and nonroutine cases, with an economy of effort.
MASTER	One who is regarded as "the" expert among experts or the "real" expert among all employees. He or she is among the elite group whose judgments are looked upon to set the standard and ideals for others.

time, they are experienced specialists. These individuals cannot yet be considered as experts by virtue of their experience alone. Chi, Glaser, and Farr (1988) say that in contrast to all other levels, experts possess an organized body of conceptual and procedural knowledge and have much experience over time. Masters are experts of the highest order, and not all experts achieve this level of competence. Jascha Heifetz, generally known as one of the most brilliant violinists of the twentieth century, once remarked when offered a university teaching position, "I hope to be good enough to teach." Such is the high regard and difficulty for experts to move to the next step to attain the master level of competence.

Being an expert means that those persons can use their high levels of competence in practical ways. That is the essential nature of expertise. One does not reach the expert level overnight. Certainly all experts first began as novices, and there were stages of development in between. The training certificates of a skilled professional—say, an auto mechanic or a physician—simply mean that he or she has completed the educational requirements necessary for doing the set of work. For a customer, the certificates signify that the job holder has the potential for providing effective service. The certificates do not guarantee that the mechanic or physician knows how to use the information that he or she has acquired or that he or she can take the appropriate actions in specific instances. From the customers' perspective, determining whether the professional is an expert depends on how the vehicle functions after the repair or how fast the patient recovers after diagnosis and treatment.

Thus, expertise almost always refers to the ability to use knowledge and skills to achieve outcomes that have value to someone else. Yet, being a *master*, *expert*, a *specialist*, or a *novice* are usually relative notions. Gilbert (1978) states that individuals who demonstrate exemplary performance or the historically best levels of performance while incurring the lowest costs in doing their work always seem to emerge in organizations. Therefore, the outcomes achieved by experts are exemplary, but *exemplary* is a standard that can change over time. This fact is seen most dramatically in organizations that have undergone major change efforts. When experts leave an organization—oftentimes for early retirement—the other employees naturally move up to use what they know and can do, even if they cannot achieve the same outcomes equal to the persons who had just departed.

Employee competence in organizations is subject to continuous change. Seven related situations occur that affect employee competence: new hires, job promotion, job rotation and transfer, continuous improvement efforts, multiskilling, technology, and change in the nature of work. While these situations have always been with us, they occur today with greater frequency, and their impact on organizational performance is potentially more crucial than it has been in the past.

New Hires: Full-time, Part-time, and Temporary Employees

As entrants into the organization, new hires have always required extra organizational attention to develop the required level of competence. Regardless of academic background or previous work experience, the new hires should be aware of the organization's policies, culture, and mission; understand the goals and requirements of their work area; and use specific areas of knowledge, skills, and attitudes to do their jobs. These are all areas of competence that the employee should develop.

Recently, fewer organizations seem to be hiring large numbers of new hires. It might seem that employee competence would be affected less by this situation. However, recent hiring patterns have only complicated the matter. Instead of relying on permanent new hires, many global organizations are now bringing in part-time and temporary employees. The Organization for Economic Cooperation and Development (OECD), an independent organization of thirty member countries sharing a commitment to democratic government and the market economy, estimates that nearly 15 percent of the U.S. labor force is employed part-time, nearly 20 percent in Germany, nearly 25 percent in Japan, and over 30 percent in the Netherlands (OECD, 2002).

As the baby-boomer generation reaches retirement age, these percentages will likely increase. Organizations face unique challenges when they employ large numbers of part-time and temporary employees. After all, temporary employees are expected to achieve the same quality and productivity outcomes.

Promotion

Promotion is another common situation that affects the collective competence of organizations. When employees are given new roles or their status is upgraded, they invariably need to acquire new areas of competence. It will take some time before these employees know and can do all the things necessary to perform at high levels in their new assignments. Once the initial elation of the promotion passes, these employees often feel much discomfort and uncertainty.

The effects of promotion on skilled technical employees who are promoted into supervisory positions are particularly evident. In their new role, these employees discover that they must perform work representing totally new areas of knowledge and skills, such as planning the work of others, providing coaching and counseling, and conducting performance feedback sessions with subordinates. These demands often cause some to wonder whether they really want to keep their new positions or return to the relative comfort of their previous positions.

Rotations and Transfers

Rotations and transfers move employees into different roles or functional areas. The new assignment can be either short-term or permanent, depending on the intent of the move. Many organizations use rotation and transfers as a planned part of the career development process. These experiences invariably place new demands on employees' knowledge and skills.

The challenge for organizations is to help these employees achieve their individual goals by giving them access to new career opportunities whenever possible, while at the same time making certain that the movement of employees does not unduly disrupt the organization's ability to achieve its goals.

Continuous Improvement Efforts

Changes in employee competence also occur as a result of continuous improvement efforts. Whenever teams of employees get together to improve how the work is done, they often result in recommendations for change. These recommendations can involve the simplification of work, use of a new tool, eliminate redundant steps in work process, or some combination of them all. When these recommendations are enacted, changes in employee competence can be expected.

Multiskilling

When the continuous improvement process suggests ways of making work more efficient, it often means that employees' responsibilities must broaden or that they must become more multiskilled (Jones & Jacobs, 1994). Many managers find that developing multiskilled employees enables them to reduce costs, improve productivity, and enrich employees' jobs. Corporate redesign has also increased the need for employees to become more multiskilled.

Multiskilling makes it possible for employees to share work or to take over for each other when work conditions permit this to be done. Multiskilling can be an effective way of increasing efficiency and productivity, but many areas of knowledge and skill are required in order for them to perform the additional tasks expected of them. How to acquire the ability to perform the new work, without lessening the individual's ability to perform their present work, remains a challenge.

Technology

Possibly the single most pervasive force affecting the competence of organizations is technology. Technology takes many forms: using a laptop computer to calculate insurance needs, managing an automated inventory control system, or operating an industrial robot on a production line. Nearly every employee has already faced or in the future will face changes in his or her work caused by the introduction of technology. The U.S. Bureau of Labor Statistics estimates that employment in information technology jobs more than doubled from 1988 to 1996. But the pool of workers with the appropriate skills has not kept pace with this demand, placing greater emphasis on organization-based training.

In fact, many organizations are now entering their second or third generation of technological change, which means that employees must make a continuous effort to develop new areas of knowledge and skills.

In one sense, today's technology is only a new generation of work tools, no different in many respects from the tools that man used in the past. But, because recent advances in technology have already caused such dramatic changes in the way work is done, many employees now expect their present levels of competence to have a relatively short life span and that they need to acquire new areas of competence on a continuous basis.

Change in the Nature of Work

Increasingly, employees are not assigned to a job with distinct sets of tasks. Instead, more and more individuals are moved from project to project, especially with those employees involved in knowledge work. Often the project team brings a variety of experiences and skills to a certain project. This rich mixture of backgrounds allows the team to tackle simple and complex projects.

When an employee joins a project team, there are some units of work that team members must perform for the first time. Simply put, they must acquire the new areas of competence in a relatively short period of time. Failure to do so will likely have an adverse impact on the entire project and the performance of the other team members. Individuals must develop new competencies as they are assigned to the projects.

To summarize, the seven situations just reviewed affect the relative level of employee competence within organizations. When employees' knowledge and skills are affected in a detrimental way, it often takes considerable time to recover. And while areas of employee competence have always been subject to change, change is more common than ever before, and the need for new areas of competence has thus increased. All these factors mean that developing the appropriate levels of human competence in the most effective and efficient ways possible is one of today's major challenges.

DEVELOPING EMPLOYEE COMPETENCE THROUGH TRAINING

Training is the primary means that organizations use to develop employee competence to the appropriate levels required. In this sense, training and employee competence go hand in hand. Whether employees need to be experts or specialists to meet work expectations, training is the means to communicate that information to others. Of course, training alone cannot instantly make an employee a high performer. Training can only help an employee achieve the specialist level of competence first of all, and the employee must make an effort over a period of time to achieve a higher status. However, achieving mastery at the specialist level is prerequisite for becoming an expert later on. And the best way of achieving mastery is through some form of structured training.

In this book, training in organizations can be distinguished by the two basic locations in which it is conducted: off the job and on the job.

Off-the-Job Training

In general, off-the-job training programs provide group-based learning opportunities on a variety of topics at a site other than where the work is actually done. Off-the-job training can be conducted in an off-site training classroom near the job setting, in an adjoining facility dedicated exclusively to training, or in a corporate or private facility located far away from the work setting. In many instances, off-the-job training requires extensive travel. Training classrooms, vestibule training setups, and specially constructed training laboratories are some examples of off-the-job training sites.

Within the past thirty years or so, the use of formal off-the-job training programs has risen dramatically. Carnevale and Gainer (1989) estimated that more than $30 billion is spent for off-the-job training programs every year. It seems difficult today to estimate with any confidence the total amount of money spent on training in organizations. However, surveys of benchmarking companies conducted by the American Society for Training and Development estimated that total training expenditures continue to increase, whether measured on a per-employee basis or as a percentage of annual payroll, upward of 37 percent between 2000 and 2001 (Van Buren & Erskine, 2001).

Although these amounts are impressive, it may still not reflect the total cost of off-the-job training. Many organizations have made sizeable investments in the construction of specialized training centers and campuslike facilities in which their training programs are conducted. Nor does the figure just cited include the costs of the human resource development staff to design, deliver, and manage the training programs conducted in these facilities. These expenses would undoubtedly increase the cost of off-the-job training programs.

Further evidence for the prevalence of off-the-job training programs comes from the American Society for Training and Development (ASTD), which publishes an annual report of the state of the human resource development industry (Van Buren & Erskine, 2001). Figure 1.1 shows that among benchmark companies, instructor-led courses in a classroom were reportedly used for the highest amount of training time. This same result has been reported in the previous five annual reports, though it is doubtful if the estimates actually represent the true picture of how learning occurs in these benchmark organizations.

On-the-Job Training (OJT)

Not all training occurs off-site. In fact, most learning occurs as a result of training that is conducted in the work setting itself, not in a training classroom (Jacobs & Osman-Gani, 1999; Wexley & Latham, 1991). In general, OJT is the process in which one person, most often the supervisor or lead person of a work area, passes job knowledge and skills to another person (Broadwell, 1986). OJT occurs at the location in which the work is done or at least closely simulating the

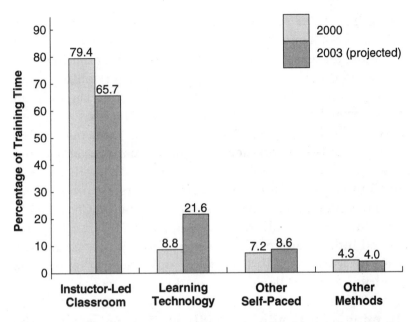

FIGURE 1.1. Use of Training Delivery Methods. *Used with permission (Van Buren & Erskine, 2001).*

work location as much as possible, and it is often thought of as involving both learning and doing at the same time.

Historically, OJT has always figured prominently in the acquisition of employee competence (Miller, 1987). After all, before there were off-site corporate training classrooms, the only way in which a person could reasonably expect to learn a profession or a trade was by working at the side of an experienced employee. For example, during the Middle Ages, apprentices worked with master craftsmen, who exercised considerable control over their work and socialization experiences, for long periods of time. During the latter part of the nineteenth century and early part of the twentieth century, OJT might be characterized by having supervisors and foremen use OJT to show new industrial workers how to operate production machinery. Today's version of OJT might be characterized by having an individual sit alongside a colleague to learn how to use a computer program or to learn how to troubleshoot a specific computer error.

Most discussions of OJT refer to the influential role that it played during the two world wars of the twentieth century. Interestingly, these two periods of immense national threat brought about the most important advances in the use of OJT. During World War I, Charles R. "Skipper" Allen drew upon his experiences as a vocational educator to devise a four-step method of delivering OJT. Supervisors used the four steps to train civilian shipbuilders, who had never before worked in an industrial environment (McCord, 1987).

While Allen's efforts were highly successful, they received little attention after the war. In fact, it wasn't until the start of World War II did a wide audience appreciate the contributions of Allen's four-step delivery process.

OJT received its greatest emphasis as a result of the Training within Industry (TWI) Service, an agency of the War Manpower Commission's Bureau of Training, which was created in 1940 and was discontinued in 1945 (Dooley, 1945). The TWI Service was directed by Channing Rice Dooley and codirected by his friend Walter Dietz. These two men possessed a unique vision on how to implement OJT in organizations involved in war production. C. R. Dooley (1882–1956) in particular believed people needed to learn by doing, but the learning should be done with a trainer highly involved in the trainee's learning process. He was famous for showing people how to tie the underwriter's knot used by electricians by placing his hand on the person's hand and guiding the person through each step of the knot-tying procedure. Dooley's eighty-two-year-old son David recently recalled his father's philosophy on training and learning: "Until you take the man's hands and say take this [end] right through there, and then they'd get it. It's really wonderful to see the man's eyes light up, and they'd realize they'd been trained" (Jacobs, 2001).

Such high involvement might not be possible in all industrial training situations, but it represented Dooley's strong beliefs about the learning process. Dooley was inducted in the Academy of Human Resource Development's Scholar Hall of Fame for his profound contributions to the HRD field.

The TWI Service's important contributions began within the first week of its existence, as a study was commissioned to try out a new way of training lens grinders. One of the most serious expertise shortages at the time was in skilled lens grinders and polishers of precision instruments, such as the optical instruments used on bombsights. During the study, a comprehensive job analysis was conducted, and a seven-step training process based on Allen's four steps was devised. These seven steps were the following:

1. Show him how to do it.

2. Explain the key points.

3. Let him watch you do it again.

4. Let him do the simple parts of the job.

5. Help him do the whole job.

6. Let him do the whole job—but watch him.

7. Put him on his own.

The lens grinder study was highly successful: Training time was reduced from the original estimate of five years to six months. Later, the amount of time to train lens grinders was further reduced. Because of the specific importance of the lens grinder study, Appendix A presents the study as it was summarized in the TWI Service final report written by Dooley in 1945.

As the TWI Service was established, the seven steps from the lens grinder study were found to be too cumbersome. Allen's original four steps were adopted as the standard for delivering OJT. Building on the success of lens grinder study, the TWI established the Job Instruction Training (JIT) program, which focused primarily on the delivery of technical skills. Possibly the most prominent aspect of JIT continues to be the Job Instruction card—a card that presents two sets of information:

1. How to Get Ready to Instruct

   Have a timetable. How much skill you expect him to have, by what date

   Break down the job. List the important steps. Pick out the key points. Safety is always a key point.

   Have everything ready. Do you have the right equipment? The right materials? The right supplies?

   Arrange the workplace properly. Is the workplace just as the trainee will be expected to keep it?

2. How to Instruct

   Prepare the worker. Put the trainee at ease. State the job and find out what the trainee knows about the job. Get the trainee interested in learning about the job. Place the trainee in the correct position.

   Present the operation. Tell, show, and illustrate each step at a time carefully and patiently. Stress each key point. Instruct clearly and completely. Include only one point at a time, but no more than the trainee can master at the time.

   Try out performance. Have the trainee perform the job, and correct errors. Have the trainee explain each key point while performing the job. Make sure that the trainee understands by asking questions and correcting errors. Continue until you are sure that the trainee has learned.

   Follow up. Put the trainee in the performance setting on his own. Assign people to be helpers along the way. Check the trainee frequently, but taper off coaching as time goes by. Praise good work and coach to correct poor work.

The job card concluded with this admonition: *If the worker hasn't learned, then the trainer hasn't taught.* The TWI Service followed up the JIT program with other programs, including Job Methods Training (JMT), Job Relations Training (JRT), Union Relations Training (URT), and Program Development. All of these programs emphasized the work setting as the primary location for delivering the training content.

Although the TWI Service was discontinued in 1945, the successes of its programs had made a lasting effect on participating organizations. In the postwar period, C. R. Dooley created the TWI Foundation in an attempt to address economic reconstruction needs through his training approach. From 1948 to 1950, Dooley served the U.S. State Department in various capacities, serving on various international boards and agencies to "spread the gospel" of the TWI approach, including some time in Paris and Geneva, Switzerland.

Recent surveys of industry training practices confirm that OJT remains the most frequently used training method for a wide range of jobs, including skilled, semiskilled, sales, supervisory, and management positions; types of organizations; and sizes of organizations (Futrell, 1988; Churchill, Ford, & Walker, 1985; Kirkpatrick, 1985; Kondrasuk, 1979; Utgaard & Davis, 1970; Rothwell & Kazanas,1990). Jacobs and Osman-Gani (1999) found that OJT is the most frequently used training approach for organizations in Singapore, across several business sectors. Rothwell and Kazanas (1990) studied the use of structured on-the-job training in various types of organizations and found that most organizations, especially manufacturing organizations, were doing a substantial amount of their training through OJT, but it was unclear whether the OJT that they had observed had been planned and delivered in a systematic manner.

Carnevale and Gainer (1989) estimate an employee learns 90 percent of his or her job knowledge and skills through OJT. Furthermore, they suggest that organizations will spend three times more per employee for OJT than for off-the-job training, and they point out that most organizations have no designated budget item for OJT. Finally, up to one-third of a new hire's first-year salary is devoted to costs of OJT.

These results confirm what most managers and employees know to be true from their practical experience: In spite of benchmarking surveys and educated guesses that indicate the prevalence of off-the-job training in organizations, most training and learning in organizations continues to take place in actual work settings, not in a training classroom.

EMERGENCE OF STRUCTURED ON-THE-JOB TRAINING

The effects of the global economy have necessarily increased the importance of training within organizations. However, while training has generally found itself in a more strategic position, this has not meant that everyone has been totally satisfied with the way it has been used. In fact, both managers and HRD professionals have expressed deep concerns about how training is carried out in their organizations (Sloman, 1989). Paradoxically, the more often training is used, the more concern seems to be expressed about it. To a large extent, the emergence of S-OJT has been a result of these concerns.

Concerns with Off-the-Job Training

At first glance, most off-the-job training programs appear to be effective, of high quality, and generally well received by trainees. By virtue of its location, an off-site training program may offer some trainees a reprieve from the pressures of the immediate work setting, which helps them focus more intently on the training content. Nevertheless, many managers recognize that, no matter what topic presented, off-the-job training programs can result in any one of the following problems:

- Employees learn what was presented in the training, but because no one else from their work area was aware of the nature of the training program, they seldom have occasion or are rewarded to use what was learned.

- Employees learn what was presented in the training, but because no one highlighted the aspects that were critical for meeting customer's needs before the training occurred, they are uncertain of the relevance of the information learned.

- Employees enjoy learning the content of the training programs and praise the programs after they return to their work area without realizing that what they have learned is different from what they practice on their jobs.

- Employees return to their work areas and discover that what they learned during the training represented only a small amount of the information that they require in order to do their jobs.

- Employees learn what was presented in the training, but because management fails to supply the follow-up required, their use of the information inevitably drops off.

As a result of these concerns, many managers have come to suspect that the goals of off-the-job training programs often contradict the organization's goals. Increasingly, training content and schedules seem unresponsive to the sponsoring organization's business needs, and training certificates take on more importance than job knowledge and skills. At the same time, many HRD professionals perceive that managers do not realize how much time is required to design effective off-the-job training programs. Nonetheless, off-the-job training programs may cost more than the value they produce for an organization.

Concerns with On-the-Job Training

OJT has been subject to different concerns. While OJT has been used more often than off-the-job training, most instances of OJT are essentially informal, which means that they occur without advance planning or involvement by management. The entire training may be placed in the hands of an individual who does not know the work, has poor work habits, or considers the training an imposition on his or her work time. Under these conditions, training takes lower priority than work, even when training might help improve the quality of the work. Most employees are forced to learn regardless of these constraints. Thus, most of the OJT programs conducted in organizations can be considered unplanned or, as described by Swanson and Sawzin (1975), unstructured in nature.

Unstructured OJT occurs when trainees learn job knowledge and skills from impromptu explanations or demonstrations by others; through trial and error efforts, self-motivated reading, or questioning on their own; or simply imitating the behaviors of others. Consider the comments of a newly hired nurse who received unstructured OJT from an experienced nurse. Her comments are representative of most employees who receive unstructured OJT:

> "When I first came on, I was trained by another nurse at the time. We became friends, more or less. I relied upon her to tell me what to do. She told me, 'Do this or don't do that. This is how I do this.' Eventually I learned what she wanted me to learn, but I found that I could learn just as well on my own. I'm not sure if I really learned what they wanted me to learn. Anyway, after a while, I just started figuring out things on my own."

Unstructured OJT has been called many things: follow Joe (or Jane) training, sink-or-swim training, sit-by-Nellie training, buddy training, learning the ropes, and do-it-yourself training, to name a few. These terms have some historical significance: *Sit-by-Nellie training* comes from learning how to operate looms in Britain during the industrial revolution. *Learning the ropes* comes from learning to understand and manipulate the maze of lines and shrouds on eighteenth-century American whaling ships. But the meaning remains even today. Anyone of working age has been subjected to this type of training at some point in his or her career and knows the frustration it can cause.

Moreover, unstructured OJT has a number of problems:

- The desired training outcomes are rarely, if ever, achieved, and when it is, all trainees rarely achieve the same outcomes.
- The training content is often inaccurate or incomplete, or else it represents an accumulation of bad habits, misinformation, and possibly unsafe shortcuts on which employees have come to rely over time.
- Experienced employees are seldom able to communicate what they know in a way that others can understand.
- Experienced employees use different methods each time they conduct the training, and not all the methods are equally effective.
- Employees are often unsure whether they are even allowed to train others, and they may say, "It's not my job."
- Many employees fear that sharing their knowledge and skills will reduce their own status as experts and possibly even threaten their job security.

Thus, while unstructured OJT occurs most often, employees seldom achieve the desired levels of competence as a result of its use. Studies have shown that unstructured OJT leads to increased error rates, lower productivity, and decreased training efficiency, compared to structured on-the-job training (Jacobs & Hruby-Moore, 1998; Jacobs, 1994; Jacobs, Jones, & Neil, 1992). Perhaps the best that can be said about unstructured OJT is that, despite its problems, most employees eventually overcome the barriers that it creates and learn at least some of what they need to know and do. Managers often believe that they can train employees and do their own work at the same time. Unfortunately, such an arrangement does not provide the basis for a positive learning experience, nor does it make for the most efficient use of organizational resources.

To summarize, off-the-job training programs are well intentioned, but they either miss the mark or are too far away from the performance setting to have an impact on employee's competence. Managers can ill afford to take employees away from their jobs each time training is required or wait patiently for the programs to be scheduled at the convenience of someone else. Moreover, most uses of unstructured OJT are ineffective in achieving the training objectives, which inhibits the achievement of important organizational outcomes.

Training should take place closer to the point of work performance. At times this means close to the customer. Demographic projections about the future workforce and its educational characteristics complicate these concerns. In 1987, Johnston and Packer asserted the need for employee training and development will become increasingly acute in the near future, in large part because a great number of individuals entering the labor market do not have the skills required for high-wage jobs. More recently, in an essay written for *The Economist*, Peter Drucker projected that the next thirty years will be characterized by the next generation, which will feature a totally new set of demographics. For instance, by 2030, people over sixty-five in Germany, the world's third largest economy, will account for almost half the adult population. The critical question is how to get far more output from those remaining in the workforce to support the pension system of those already retired (Drucker, 2001).

In 2000, the Social Security Administration reported that labor force participation had reached its highest proportion ever in the United States. More than 30 percent of the labor force has a college degree. Over 75 percent of women are now working. And employers need even more people to fill job openings. The number of those individuals entering the labor force from 2000 to 2020 aged twenty-five to fifty-four is expected to grow by only 3 percent. As a result, many employers have been forced to lure even more people into the workforce, such as hard-to-place workers (welfare recipients, people with disabilities, immigrants) and individuals with low skills.

The conjunction of these organizational and societal issues has motivated the continuing interest in S-OJT. Although S-OJT is not a panacea, it has the potential for developing employee competence effectively and efficiently, even in the most difficult economic times. For many organizations, the challenge today is that of survival in an economic era that emphasizes the quality of products and services; cooperation between employees, management, and unions; and high efficiency (Kaufman & Jones, 1990).

This book seeks to help organizations respond to these challenges, through the ongoing development of employees to achieve the highest levels of competence possible.

CONCLUSION

Expertise is important for organizations that seek to meet the challenges of the global economy. Although the expert level of competence might not be necessary in all instances, it is important to develop employees to the appropriate levels of competence. Managers and HRD professionals recognize that off-the-job training programs often do not have the desired relevance and that on-the-job training efforts are usually ineffective. The interest in S-OJT has emerged in this context.

Chapter 2
A System View of Structured On-the-Job Training

Much of the increased interest in S-OJT comes from its greater efficiency and effectiveness compared to unstructured forms of OJT. This chapter builds an understanding of S-OJT by viewing it from a system perspective. Topics covered in this chapter include:

- the meaning of S-OJT,
- the system view to S-OJT, and
- the three defining features of S-OJT.

THE MEANING OF STRUCTURED ON-THE-JOB TRAINING

As far as can be determined, Jacobs and McGiffin (1987) make the first reference to *structured* on-the-job training as a unique form of training. Many authors before them, including Goldstein (1974) and Connor (1983), had suggested the need for more structured forms of OJT, but they were the first to differentiate it clearly from unstructured OJT. As stated in Chapter 1, OJT received a great deal of attention during both world wars, but today's efforts to improve OJT are driven by challenges of a different sort. Today, managers must find ways of combating the effects of changing market demands, advanced technologies, and lowering production and service delivery costs.

Interest in structured on-the-job training can be confirmed by the references to it in the professional literature and its recognitions. For instance, recent texts on the topic include Walter (2002); Sisson (2001); Lawson (1997); Pike, Solem, and Arch (2000); Rothwell and Kazanas (1994); and Ramsey (1993). Semb, Ellis, Fitch, Parchman, and Irick (1995) present a model of how to conduct on-the-job training and assessed practices aboard Navy ships. Jacobs (2002) describes a series of case studies that show how practitioners from various national and international organizations have implemented planned training programs on the job. Jacobs (2001) edited a monograph in which authors described a range of theoretical and practical issues related to planned training on the job.

Finally, the Weirton Steel Company was recognized for its use of structured on-the-job training by the Best Manufacturing Practices Center of Excellence. The BMPCOE is a partnership among the Office of Naval Research, the Department of Commerce, and the University of Maryland, to identify and validate best industry practices, document them, and encourage industry, government, and academia to share information about them.

Organizations refer to their structured on-the-job training programs in a number of different ways, including task training, buddy training, training on the job, on-the-job coaching, and planned OJT. Absent from the literature several years ago, structured on-the-job training, under one or another of its several names, is now a generally recognized form of training available in many organizations.

S-OJT is defined as:

The planned process of developing competence on units of work by having an experienced employee train a novice employee at the work setting or a location that closely resembles the work setting.

This definition makes four points clear. First, like other planned training approaches, S-OJT achieves training objectives reliably and predictably. Second, the training occurs for the expressed purpose of passing along the ability to perform specific units of work or tasks. The term *unit of work* refers to the discrete sets of behaviors and outcomes that characterize what all people do on their jobs, ranging from front-line employees to senior managers. S-OJT is not about learning to perform an entire job but a subset of the job.

Third, S-OJT emphasizes that the training will occur on a one-on-one basis. In practice, S-OJT might necessarily involve several trainees with a single trainer. However, even in these circumstances, there remains close contact between trainer and trainee. Research has shown unique benefits of having direct learner contact with an instructor over group instruction methods or self-instructional approaches that use printed materials or automated devices (Bloom, 1984).

S-OJT takes full instructional advantage of this immediate level of social contact. Simply put, learning is fundamentally a human process. The benefits of individuals being in direct contact with each other has yet to be surpassed by any other means of delivering training.

Fourth, the definition specifies that the training will occur where the work is actually done or in a setting that is similar to the work setting. This aspect about S-OJT distinguishes it from most other training approaches. It would be too limiting to say that S-OJT *must* occur in the actual work setting every time it is used. In practice, S-OJT has been used in training labs in training centers, simulators in off-site facilities, or designated training areas near the work setting. Thus, S-OJT can occur in the actual work setting or in an alternate setting that provides all the critical attributes—that is, the same environment, the same cues, and the same response demands—of the work setting.

VIEWING S-OJT AS A SYSTEM

S-OJT differs from unstructured OJT in making use of a planned process. Carrying out the planned process with a system view helps ensure that the training will be efficient and effective. No other theoretical framework for instruction and performance improvement can make that promise (Jacobs, 1989). The system view maintains that all natural and artificial entities are systems and that the behavior of systems is relatively predictable, which means that systems can be designed and managed with some confidence.

This era of unpredictable change makes the argument for systems thinking even more compelling (Senge, 1990). Patterns inevitably emerge that help us explain present events and predict future events. For managers, systems thinking is sometimes as simple as recognizing that if you push on one side of the organization, the opposite side is likely to move, too, but in the opposite direction. Managers should use what they know about the system at hand to respond in informed ways to the reactions observed.

The system view also helps us distinguish between the means and ends of our actions. Every training approach, including S-OJT, is merely a means to an end, not an end in itself. The use of S-OJT is not the ultimate goal when using S-OJT. Rather, S-OJT is one way of improving organizational performance, because it helps develop appropriate levels of employee competence. When employees have these abilities, they can increase productivity, complete projects on time, lower defect rates, or achieve other outcomes of importance. These are the outcomes that matter for organizations, and the effectiveness of S-OJT should always be judged from this perspective.

The system view has two basic implications for S-OJT. First, it says that S-OJT is a system composed of several interacting parts that work together to achieve common goals

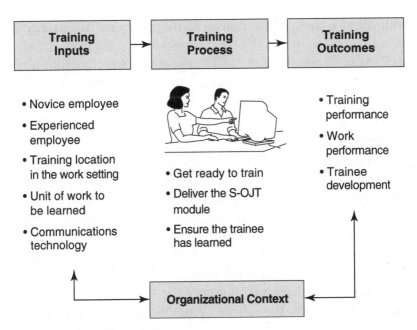

FIGURE 2.1. The S-OJT System

(Jacobs, 1989; Rummler & Brache, 1995). Second, it says that S-OJT should be developed and implemented systematically.

The two implications interrelate in fundamental ways. The S-OJT process guides how S-OJT is put together regardless of the nature of the work. To improve the training with greater precision, S-OJT should be thought of as a functioning system.

The S-OJT System

Figure 2.1 shows the training inputs, training process, and training outputs implied in the view of S-OJT as a system. It also shows that the system components are affected by the organizational context in which the system exists. This perspective may be puzzling to some readers who see OJT simply as a purposeful conversation between two or more employees. However, the training event is more than the social interactions. In fact, S-OJT represents the interaction of several parts that are essential for ensuring the success of the system.

Training Inputs

The training inputs of S-OJT include the people involved, the training location in the work setting necessary to conduct the training, the information about the unit of work to be learned, and the communications technology that might be used to deliver information about the work.

The first input in the system is the novice employee who lacks the appropriate level of competence to perform the unit of work and who is therefore the trainee. For the training to be effective, the *novice employee* should possess:

- the prerequisites needed to learn the training content and

- the personality and temperament that is best suited for the training approach.

The next input is the experienced employee who functions as the trainer. The *experienced employee* should have a combination of:

- appropriate competence in the unit of work and

- appropriate competence as a trainer.

The term *experienced employee* is preferred to *expert employee* because the individual who has the highest level of competence is not always the best trainer. The best trainer combines competence in the unit of work and in training.

The third input is *training location* in the work setting in which S-OJT is to occur. The *training location* should provide:

- the resources required to conduct the training,
- minimal conflicts with ongoing production or service delivery, and
- an atmosphere conducive for training and learning.

As stated in the definition, S-OJT may not occur in the work setting where the work is to be performed. In these cases, the training location that is selected should be suited to achieve the training objectives.

The fourth training input is the *unit of work* that is to be learned. More than most other training approaches, S-OJT focuses on relatively small units of work, such as tasks, projects, and special assignments. Training objectives, which describe the predicted abilities of the trainee at the conclusion of the training, are defined in terms of the specific work unit that is to be learned. The *unit of work* should be:

- selected as being suited for S-OJT,
- analyzed into the component parts,
- related to training objectives and other important information, and
- combined with other information in the form of a training module.

The last training input is the *communications technology* that might be used to store, deliver, and manage information about the training. This training input has been added to the model because of the emerging use of knowledge management systems, wireless receivers, and other computer devices that allow new possibilities in how S-OJT is managed and delivered. The first edition of this text assumed (as did most readers) that the training would be delivered to the trainee via text-based information on the printed page with the trainer alongside the trainee. Increasingly, communications technology has become a distinct system element to the S-OJT system, causing many to rethink, in part, the fundamental relationship between the trainer and trainee during S-OJT. Thus, because of its emerging and future impact, *communications* technology warrants inclusion as a training input.

Training Process

In the process component of S-OJT, the trainer delivers the module to the trainee, who is expected to learn the content. Thus, the actions of the trainer before, during, and after he or she delivers the training to a large extent determine the effectiveness of the training. The training process includes:

- the trainer's actions to get ready to train,
- the trainer's actions in using the training events to deliver the S-OJT module, and
- the trainer's actions to ensure that the trainee has learned.

Training Outputs

The training outputs occur as a result of combining the training inputs during the training process. The training outputs include the ability of the novice employee to:

- perform at the end of the training to meet the requirements of the training objectives,
- perform the work to the level required by the job expectations, and
- achieve his or her development goals.

Logically, the primary output of any training system is the achievement of the training objectives. However, achievement of the training objectives cannot be judged in isolation from the other possible outcomes of the system. Do the training objectives address the needs of the individual employee and the organization? Remember that the business needs of the organization were what motivated the use of S-OJT in the first place.

Organizational Context

Finally, as a system, S-OJT exists within a larger context. In effect, S-OJT is a system in direct contact with other, sometimes conflicting, systems, such as the work system. Thus, the various components of the S-OJT system are subject to the influences from issues that emerge from the organizational context. These are some of the major issues that affect S-OJT:

- Business and priorities facing the organization, such as reducing personnel costs, improving quality, or increasing market share
- The nature of ongoing change efforts, such as company-wide productivity studies, process improvement programs, or safety programs
- Perceptions of the value of training that prevail among senior management, supervisors, and employees
- Contractual agreements between management and unions that prohibit some line employees from serving as trainers
- Alignment between training and organizational objectives
- Alignment between work expectations and the consequences of using experienced employees as trainers
- Willingness of line and staff functions to manage and maintain S-OJT after it has been implemented

The S-OJT Process

Figure 2.2 presents the second implication of the system view—namely, that an orderly process is needed for the design, delivery, and evaluation of S-OJT. In general, the six process steps shown are the ones that allow us to put together a system in the most effective and efficient ways possible. In that sense, the process shown is ideal. It often has to be adapted in practice to fit the demands of new situations. Often, steps in the process are interactive and iterative,

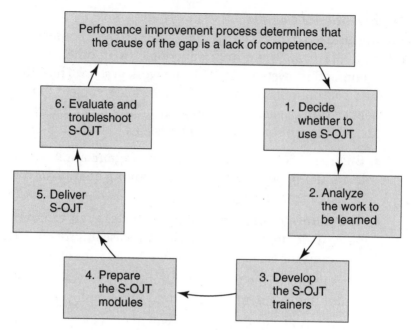

FIGURE 2.2. The S-OJT Process

which means that information from one step affects other steps and that steps can be repeated as learning occurs during the process.

The S-OJT process should be considered a subset of the larger performance improvement process. As such, S-OJT process should be used only after a thorough analysis of the gap between the current/anticipated and the desired performance outcomes. As stated, S-OJT is appropriate only when the cause of the gap is caused by a lack of appropriate employee competence to perform as expected. Readers unfamiliar with the topics of needs assessment or performance analysis should consult Kaufman (2000), Rossett (1987), Kaufman and Zahn (1993), and Harless (1978).

The S-OJT process has six steps:

1. *Decide whether to use S-OJT.* The first step in the process is to determine whether it is appropriate to

use S-OJT for the unit of work at hand. To perform this step, you should have knowledge of the instructional features of S-OJT and of specific selection criteria.

2. *Analyze the units of work to be learned.* Once you have identified the units of work that are appropriate to be learned through S-OJT, you should analyze the information to derive the training content and outcomes. Some design processes place work analysis before the selection of the training approach. The order is reversed because it is assumed that an inventory is available when the process begins. If an inventory is not available, then the units of work should be identified before selecting the training approach.

3. *Develop the S-OJT trainers.* S-OJT is effective only when experienced or knowledgeable employees serve as trainers. Trainers should have both appropriate levels of competence in the unit of work and in being a trainer. Developing S-OJT trainers is a process unto itself.

4. *Prepare the S-OJT modules.* The training content and other important information should be assembled into a S-OJT module. At this point, considerations for the appropriate use of communications technology need to be undertaken. The module guides the trainer while he or she delivers the training, and the trainee uses it for reference during the training.

5. *Deliver S-OJT.* Before delivering the training, the trainer must do everything that he or she needs to do to get ready to train. Then, the trainer delivers the training in a way consistent with the type of training involved: managerial, technical, or awareness. Delivery is guided by the five training events:

   a. Prepare the trainee.

   b. Present the training.

    c. Require a response.

    d. Provide feedback.

    e. Evaluate performance.

How these training events are used depends on the type of training.

6. *Evaluate and troubleshoot S-OJT.* The various outcome, process, and input components should be evaluated in light of the performance expectations. Any unanticipated effects must also be evaluated. Troubleshooting involves the matching of problems and causes. This information helps us develop suggestions for action. Evaluation and troubleshooting should be done on a continuous basis.

DEFINING FEATURES OF S-OJT

Most organizations use an array of training approaches. For instance, Web-based training has been emphasized recently. Despite the many advances in training delivery, the effectiveness of any given training approach still depends on three features: (1) the amount of time that elapses between training events, (2) the match between the training setting and work setting, and (3) the learning context.

Time between Training Events

As shown in Figure 2.3, the time between training events can be thought of as the sum of the time between the presentation of the training content (A) and the trainee's opportunity to actively respond to the content (B) and the feedback from the trainer about the adequacy of the response (C). In general, a trainee learns the training content more efficiently when training events occur close together than when they are relatively spread apart (Gagne, Briggs, & Wager, 1988; Wexley, 1988).

Stuctured on-the-job training

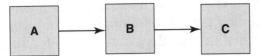

Most off-the-job training approaches

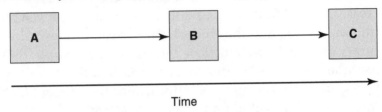

Time

FIGURE 2.3. Training Effectiveness Increases as Delay between Training Events Decreases

Clearly, S-OJT matches or beats most other training approaches, especially classroom-based training, in its potential to reduce the amount of time between the training events. This potential is a function of the one-on-one contact that occurs during training and of the fact that training is located in the work setting. Most trainers have long known that it is important to give trainees an opportunity to use what they have learned as soon as possible. Some refer to it simply as the opportunity to learn by doing at the same time (Black & Bottenberg, 1973).

Match between Training Setting and Work Setting

The benefits that accrue from reducing time between the training events are enhanced by the potential of S-OJT to provide learning experiences that closely match or in fact duplicate the behaviors that are required in the work setting (Hoffman, 1997). *Transfer of training* is the process of using what one has learned in one situation in other situations, which can differ in some respects from the situation in which the learning took place (Baldwin & Ford, 1988; Broad & Newstrom, 1992). It is often the most critical concern of managers who send their people to training. Will trainees be able to use the information that they learn after attending a training program?

Figure 2.4 shows that the transfer of training increases as the match between the training setting and work setting increases. In S-OJT, there is usually a close match between the training setting and the work setting, because the work setting is used as the training location. In many instances, S-OJT uses the very same equipment and tools that the trainee will be expected to use after the training. For this reason, S-OJT increases the potential for transfer of training.

Increasingly, researchers distinguish between near and far transfer of training (Kim & Lee, 2001). *Near transfer of training* is when there is a close match between the training content and the unit of work. As stated, S-OJT provides this level of match, perhaps better than any other training approach. *Far transfer* is when there is an approximate match

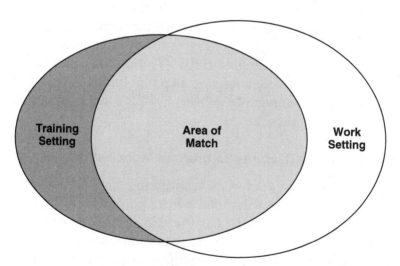

FIGURE 2.4. Training Transfer Requires a Close Match between the Training Setting and Work Setting

TABLE 2.1. Comparing Types of Units of Work and Transfer of Training		
	TRANSFER OF TRAINING	
	Near	*Far*
ESTABLISHED	The training seeks to be as close as possible to the unit of work.	The training seeks to represent critical aspects of related units of work.
	Example: Install a tire on a car.	*Example*: Install tires on a variety of vehicles.
VARYING	The training seeks to show the different patterns of using known information.	The training seeks to represent the underlying patterns of related units of work.
	Example: Conduct a customer sales presentation to sell tires.	*Example*: Conduct a customer sales presentation across a range of retail products.

Units of Work (row label spanning ESTABLISHED and VARYING)

Adapted from Lee, Kim, and Jacobs (2002).

between the training content and a related unit of work. Far transfer has intriguing possibilities for organizations because it can reduce the amount of training conducted—one training program can apply to more than one situation—and it seems to make better use of the human ability to generalize instances of concepts.

As Table 2.1 shows, Lee, Kim, and Jacobs (2002) suggest that units of work can be considered as being either established or varying and the transfer of training can be considered near or far. The resulting matrix defines each of the cells and shows a sample training module that would represent the respective cells. S-OJT has traditionally been placed in the established-near cell and perhaps in the varying-near cell. Both of these cells concern training on known sets of information. The future challenge of S-OJT is to address training topics in the established-far and varying-far cells.

Learning in the Work Context

Several researchers suggest that use of the work setting for learning can have a qualitative difference in the learning outcomes (Hart-Landsberg, Braunger, Reder, & Cross, 1992; Brown, Collins, & Duguid, 1989). Lave and Wenger (1991) argue that context-based learning is superior because it occurs in an environment that is connected to the information being presented.

In a sense, the learning becomes situated in a more relevant context. As a result, the information and the environment interact in ways that tend to strengthen each other (Stein, 2001). Situated learning challenges the assumption that cognition is independent of the context in which it occurs. Instead, situated learning suggests that the context is an integral part of the learning and, in turn, the learning is an integral part of the context.

CONCLUSION

S-OJT is the planned process of developing competence on specific units of work by having an experienced employee train a novice employee at the actual work setting or at a setting that closely simulates the work setting. The system view of S-OJT has two major implications: First, S-OJT is a system in itself. Second, S-OJT should be developed and used systematically. The two defining features of S-OJT distinguish it from most other training approaches that organizations use in the work setting.

Chapter 3
Training and Learning in the Work Setting

Structured on-the-job training represents one of many possible training approaches that organizations can use to facilitate employee learning. Increasingly, distinctions are being made between the training and learning processes that occur in organizations. This chapter:

- identifies ways that learning occurs in the work setting,
- distinguishes between informal and formal learning, and
- discusses the emergence of just-in-time training.

WAYS OF LEARNING IN THE WORK SETTING

Chapter 1 discussed concerns about the use of on-the-job training in organizations. Specifically, the chapter outlined issues in using unstructured, or unplanned, forms of OJT. OJT is not the only way that individuals could learn to perform work. Indeed, learning is an ongoing human process, and structured on-the-job training could account for only a relatively small part of what people actually learn in the course of their workdays.

	Job Instruction	Apprentice-ship	Inquiry	Self-Evaluation
TABLE 3.1. Typology of Planned Training on the Job				
LEARNING PROCESS	Systematic skills training	Socializa-tion and modeling	Analysis and problem solving	Feedback and reflection
TRAINEE'S ROLE	Applica-tion and practice	Participa-tion and observation	Exploration and orientation	Goal set-ting and evaluation
TRAINER'S ROLE	Instructor	Master and model	Tutor	Coach
Adapted from DeJong, Thijssen, and Versloot (2001).				

DeJong, Thijssen, and Versloot (2001) propose a typology of planned training on the job from the perspective of four training models: job instruction, apprenticeship, inquiry, and self-evaluation. As Table 3.1 shows, the training models can be compared by the learning process they foster, the trainee's role during the training, and the trainer's role. The intent of the typology is to begin to codify the complexity of planned training on the job.

Table 3.2 compares the unstructured and structured forms of three ways of learning in the work setting. Self-directed discovery assumes that the employee will be able to learn using his or her own devices during the course of doing the work. When the self-directed discovery is unstruc-tured, the training can be said to be trial-and-error learning or learning by doing. All work experience contains some el-ements of unstructured self-discovery learning, such as the situation when an office worker needs to replace the ink car-tridge on the new photocopier. The individual combines knowledge about how to do this same task in other ma-chines with some hypothesizing about how the cartridge

	Self-Directed Discovery	Coaching	On-the-Job Training
TABLE 3.2. Ways of Learning Information in the Work Setting			
UNSTRUCTURED	Employee learns by doing, with limited information intentionally placed in the work setting to guide learning. Employee must figure out each part of the work without any assistance. False assumptions and errors are the result.	Employee learns by working alongside or nearby an experienced employee, who seldom knows exactly how or when to intervene as the work is performed.	Employee is trained by an experienced employee, whose experience as a trainer is likely to be limited and whose understanding of the work may also be questionable. Training content, methods, and outcomes vary across employees trained.
STRUCTURED	Employee learns while doing, using the information engineered into the work setting to guide learning. Employee can trust the system to help make the learning easier and reduce frustration.	Employee learns by doing alongside or nearby an experienced employee, who uses systematic knowledge of the work to know when and how to intervene. Coaching outcomes are relatively predictable.	Employee is trained by an experienced employee who has appropriate competence in the work and in being an OJT trainer. Training content, methods, and outcomes are consistent across employees trained.

might fit into the new machine. In the end, the cartridge is installed successfully, but not without taking additional time to do it and possibly having destroyed one or two cartridges along the way. The person will likely be able to do the task without much difficulty the next time.

The structured use of self-directed discovery relies on embedded job performance guides or electronic performance support systems. To continue the prior example, most photocopier machines now have brightly labeled numbers, arrows, or other indicators to guide how to perform the task. The intent is to allow any person in the office to install the ink cartridge—whether or not that employee has previous experience with the task. More and more systems contain such embedded information with the intent of reducing operator error.

Coaching assumes that the employee can perform some, but not all, of the work being done. At some point, another employee provides information to the trainee to point out ways of improving on specific work behaviors already learned. When coaching is unstructured, the trainee works alongside others, who—it is hoped—will somehow know when and how to intervene. At times, unstructured coaching might be interpreted as meddling in another person's business.

When coaching sessions are structured, the expectations for giving and receiving information are clearly established up front. That is, the coach knows how and when to intervene during the employee's performance, and the employee knows to expect to receive some additional work information along the way.

In contrast to self-directed discovery and coaching, on-the-job training assumes that the employee lacks the competence entirely to perform the work. Most work is far more complex than installing ink cartridges in photocopiers, and the consequences of error are greater than having soiled fingers or a wasted cartridge. In those instances, having the trainee perform the work while learning it can be risky.

The structured form of on-the-job training, which is the focus of this book, is used in those instances where the unit of work is more complex than what can be learned through self-directed discovery and the employee has no previous knowledge about the work. At times, distinguishing among self-directed discovery, coaching, and OJT can be difficult in

. practice. These various ways of learning new information are often used in combination.

INFORMAL AND FORMAL LEARNING IN THE WORKPLACE

Another perspective about learning in the workplace comes from the distinction made between formal and informal types of learning. Specifically, informal learning has attracted increasing interest among researchers and organization managers in the past decade. Informal workplace learning has been defined as that learning that has not been determined by the organization (Aring, 1998). Based on this definition, S-OJT would foster formal learning because the training is largely purposeful and goal oriented, and it has defined boundaries set by the organization from the beginning to the ending. Marsick and Volpe (1999), among others, have made the point that formal learning alone cannot address all the learning needs of organizations. Instead, there is a need for organizations to foster more informal learning among employees.

Discussions about informal learning emphasize the difference between training and learning. *Training* is the external information that is presented to individuals for them to respond to. *Learning* is the internal process by which the individuals change as a result of the information they take in. Thus, on-the-job training and the on-the-job learning differ in their meanings, though they are closely related. On-the-job *learning* focuses on the process by which individuals take in information. On-the-job *training* is one means to promote on-the-job *learning*, but there can be many ways, such as peer learning, discussions, practice sessions, team learning, and experiential learning, among others.

Informal learning is a perspective both on how knowledge is generated and on organizational practice. As a perspective

on knowledge, informal learning suggests that postmodern
conditions prevalent in organizations, such as globalization,
deregulation, complexity, and flatter organization structures,
call for a different set of assumptions about knowledge (Garrick, 1998). The fundamental point is that competency-
based training approaches and reliance on experts, such as
with S-OJT, seem inherently ill suited within the context of
emerging organizational structures that require fluidity, flexibility, and dynamic approaches. Indeed, structured training
might be viewed as a negative force by exerting excessive
power and seeking employee compliance—issues that run
counter to the needs of contemporary organizations. In contrast, informal learning is said to become a source of empowerment for employees.

Informal learning as an organizational practice suggests
that since learning naturally occurs in organizations, understanding how it happens and what can be done about it goes
far in cultivating a learning environment (Aring, 1998;
Stamps, 1998). Informal learning is what is experienced and
discovered within the context of working, such as during
meetings, customer interactions, supervision, mentoring,
and peer-to-peer interactions.

As the term suggests, informal learning is noninstitu-
tional in nature but occurs continuously nevertheless (Marsick & Watkins, 1990). Informal learning fulfills many
learning needs that formal learning opportunities cannot
possibly address.

Organizations are said to suffer when informal learning
is constrained—either through a restrictive organizational
culture or through an overreliance on formal learning. As a
result, Marsick and Volpe (1999) suggest the need to design
organizational environments that foster informal learning.
Table 3.3 shows the characteristics of informal learning and
associated strategies to encourage each characteristic to
occur in organizations.

TABLE 3.3. Informal Learning Characteristics and Organizational Strategies

Characteristics	Organizational Strategies
Is integrated with work and daily routines	Make time and space for learning during work.
Is triggered by an internal or external jolt	Scan external and internal environments.
Is not highly conscious	Increase employees' awareness that learning will occur during work.
Is haphazard and influenced by chance	Attend to goals and turning points throughout work.
Is an inductive process of reflection and action	Increase inductive mind-sets and reflective skills.
Is linked to learning of others	Increase dependence on collaboration and build trust.

Adapted from Marsick and Volpe (1999).

Paradoxically, in spite of their differing end points, proponents of both informal learning and S-OJT make the same two points to support their positions. First, learning occurs on a continuous basis in organizations and the learning needs to be recognized and encouraged for the long-term benefit of both organizations and the individuals involved. Second, formal learning that occurs off the job cannot possibly address all the learning needs of individuals and organizations. Clearly, the departure point from these two topics is what should be done next.

Aside from the philosophical issues raised by some proponents of informal learning, informal learning and S-OJT are not in opposition from each other. Indeed, they are complementary, in the same way that formal and informal learning complement each other. It is encouraging to see case studies of informal learning that describe how S-OJT was used in response to issues identified through the informal learning strategies (e.g., Vernon, 1999) and structured approaches to communities of practice (Maxwell & Mosely, 2002).

Chapter 5 discusses another unanticipated informal learning outcome from implementing S-OJT. That is, it often helps the trainee and the trainer learn how to look at work in a new way. Both learn how to detect the logical parts of a unit of work. By identifying the logic of work, they have the opportunity to apply those insights in other situations.

JUST-IN-TIME TRAINING

An emerging need in organizations is to make learning and working even more seamless than ever before—that is, how to deliver training programs more strategically to trainees (Jones, 2001). Much of this issue has to do with the management of training programs such that trainees receive the right training content, at the right time, and in the right amount. S-OJT has been used to address aspects of these issues, but the issues seem larger than what S-OJT can handle alone. Thus, the term *just-in-time training* has become more prevalent in the human resource development literature.

Just-in-time training has been identified as one of the top three trends for the workplace by the Future Trends Conference sponsored by the American Society for Training and Development and the Academy of Human Resource Development (Bierema, Bing, & Carter, 2002). Just-in-time is based on its original use in manufacturing settings as expressed by Taiichi Ohno in the 1970s to establish what has become known as the Toyota production system. It was conceived as a means to more efficiently use limited organizational resources (Billesbach, 1991). In a general sense, just-in-time implies a system whereby in a short period of time, a new product is identified and a demand is generated, just enough raw materials are brought to the factory to make the product, and just enough of the new products are produced to be balanced against the customer demand. The general principles involved in just-in-time nevertheless have had a powerful influence on organizational functioning.

Just-in-time systems were first implemented in manufacturing and production organizations to help coordinate the subprocesses that converge into a single process to assemble a final product. More recently, just-in-time concepts have been used in service-related organizations to manage project activities and to ensure timely service delivery. Thus, just-in-time has moved from a manufacturing concept to a more broad management approach in organizations.

Just-in-time training describes the collective of training approaches that present a defined set of information—most of the time in the work setting—to be used by employees immediately following the training (Jones, 2001). This definition suggests three points. First, just-in-time training is planned training. Second, just-in-time training includes only the information necessary to perform at a point in time and at a specific location. Third, just-in-time training combines different training approaches to achieve its goal. For instance, just-in-time training might use S-OJT, a self-paced training package, a set of reference materials, a Web-based module, or even a classroom presentation if an appropriate number of employees have the same need for the information.

In predicting future trends, just-in-time training mostly encourages the use of electronic media to deliver the training, such as wireless communications or the Internet. The use of electronic media seems especially advantageous given the prevalence of the World Wide Web in many organizations (e.g., Fry & Barnard, 2002). Electronic media also allow the potential to deliver training, with access to large sets of information, in training situations and locations that would have been impossible otherwise. The use of electronic media has made it possible to address the organizational need.

Consider the case of a large automotive company that was required to undergo an audit of its work processes to ensure compliance with customer standards. An internal audit team was formed from three plants, with the expectation that team members would participate for staggered one-year terms. Team members held various jobs, such as engineers, accountants, front-line supervisors, and other entry-level managerial positions.

One unique challenge was the diversity of work processes the team auditors were required to review. Auditing the installation of an engine required a different set of skills than auditing the succession planning process. Another challenge was that the audit team members were located at three separate facilities. Travel expenses alone would be cost-prohibitive for the audit team to attend several training sessions at one site.

Audit team members were required to complete self-paced modules at their respective locations using the organization's wide area network immediately before they were required to complete a particular type of audit. A coach then followed the trainees from each plant while they performed a simulated audit. The coach used a checklist to ensure that all the key parts of the audit were performed.

A key aspect was that the training and follow-up coaching was done just before the actual audit was to be conducted. Thus, the training system was delivered just in time to the work performance.

CONCLUSION

This chapter discussed the ways that individuals can be trained in the work setting, besides the use of S-OJT. It also described the relationship between S-OJT and informal learning. They are distinct but complementary concepts for the benefit of individuals and organizations. Finally, the chapter introduced just-in-time training as an emerging training approach and how it relates to S-OJT.

PART TWO

STRUCTURED ON-THE-JOB TRAINING PROCESS

This part of the book presents the steps of the S-OJT process. The process should be thought of as part of the overall performance improvement process within the organization. The decision to engage in this process must be supported by a documented business issue of importance that is caused by a lack of appropriate level of competence to perform the work as expected. If it is not, the training is likely to waste scarce organizational resources.

Chapter 4
Deciding Whether to Use Structured On-the-Job Training

One part of any decision to use S-OJT is becoming aware of the ways in which it can be used. Another is determining what conditions are appropriate for its use. This chapter focuses on deciding when to use S-OJT, by examining these parts of the decision-making process:

- Four ways to use S-OJT
- S-OJT and communications technology
- Five selection factors

WAYS OF USING S-OJT

An organization can use S-OJT to present a single training program, to present training programs as related sets of work, to present training programs related to a work process or set of operations, and to present a training program in combination with off-the-job training. Or, these four ways can be combined. For example, a series of S-OJT modules related to a work process can be used in combination with off-the-job training programs. S-OJT is seldom used in isolation of other training experiences.

Single Training Program

Possibly the most common way of using S-OJT is as a single training program that addresses a specific unit of work. In this way, S-OJT modules are often used strategically. That is, trainees receive training precisely at the time when they need to learn the information.

For example, most employee grievances in the financial services division of a large insurance company were directed at newly promoted supervisors. The grievance process is time-consuming, disruptive, and costly to the organization. Employees' reasons for initiating grievances vary, but a performance analysis showed that many grievances were the result of supervisors' attempts to give performance feedback to subordinate employees.

To address the cost of grievances, giving subordinate feedback was removed from the existing managerial training program and then converted to an S-OJT module. Experienced supervisors, who were recognized for their ability to give effective feedback to subordinate employees, were asked to conduct the S-OJT. Newly promoted supervisors were assigned to an experienced supervisor to receive training on this topic. The results showed that trainees were better able to demonstrate the performance feedback process after the S-OJT than trainees had been able after the classroom based managerial.

In a manufacturing organization, the quality of the work produced by employees who had received S-OJT was compared with the quality of work of employees who had received unstructured OJT. Several inspection points on the finished product were linked to specific tasks that employees did on the production line. Work quality was assessed as number of defects made over a year's time. The results showed that, at least at one inspection point, S-OJT led to higher-quality work. In fact, the reduced defect rates saved the organization more than $20,000 in rework costs (Jacobs, 1994).

Multiple Training Programs

S-OJT has also been used to present multiple training programs related to more than one unit of work. In this way, several S-OJT modules are developed. Each module addresses a specific competency. Together, the modules can be thought of as a curriculum. Often, trainees progress through the modules in a specified sequence.

For example, a large regional bank uses S-OJT to give new and experienced tellers an understanding of a large number of financial products suitable for retail customers. It also used S-OJT to train tellers in the skills to sell the products. As part of their work, tellers are expected, when appropriate, to suggest and explain the products to customers. The bank reported that tellers are now meeting group sales goals and that several tellers had used this experience to boost their efforts to be promoted to higher-level customer service positions in the bank.

The quality control testing laboratory of an edible oil–processing company uses S-OJT to prepare newly hired lab technicians to perform eighteen basic lab tests. Lab technicians are key players in the refining process, since the results of their inspections are used to determine whether the product is ready for the next step of the process. S-OJT was conducted by supervisors during off-peak times and after hours. Training time was reduced from twelve weeks to three weeks (Jacobs & McGiffin, 1987).

Chapter 13 discusses how structured on-the-job training has been used for apprenticeships for individuals seeking to enter a certain occupation. Apprenticeships are often composed of a series of S-OJT modules.

Training Programs Related to a Work Process

Increasingly, S-OJT is being used to present training related to units of work within a work process or operation. Often, the work is done within one or more adjoining work areas. In this way, many employees can receive cross-training on many different areas of process.

For example, a manufacturer of nutritional supplements and infant formula has streamlined the customer order process to reduce the number of employees to whom large institutional customers must be referred when their purchasing agents call to inquire about orders. Telephone sales agents, contract specialists, and account managers were trained on a core set of tasks, which included determining shipment schedules, identifying shipment locations for individual products, and calculating volume discounts. The results of S-OJT showed that customers' inquiries were being addressed with significantly fewer telephone "bounces" than they had before the organization adopted the process perspective.

In a manufacturing organization with union representation, S-OJT helped team members cross-train each other on the operation, troubleshooting, and maintenance of various production and inspection equipment in their work areas. The results showed that, after S-OJT, all of the fifteen team members could operate all the various pieces of equipment in their work areas within three weeks. Before the training, each team member could operate only one piece of equipment, and none could use the sophisticated testing equipment used to inspect the parts. The results also indicated that S-OJT was five times more efficient in achieving the training objectives than the previously used unstructured OJT, when trainees were required to operate one piece of equipment only (Jacobs, Jones, & Neil, 1992).

Blended with Off-the-Job Training

Finally, S-OJT has been used as a follow-up or blended with off-the-job training programs. Such combinations recognize that group-based training can be better suited than S-OJT to achieve some training objectives, while S-OJT is better suited to achieve other training objectives.

For example, KLM Royal Dutch Airlines uses group-based training in a classroom to present the basics of customer service for newly hired cabin attendants who will serve on overseas flights. HRD staff have found that asking trainees to practice using customer service concepts on peer trainees and hired actors severely limits the effectiveness of the training, even when the classroom is designed to look like the inside of a commercial airliner, with airline seats, kitchen bays, service trolleys, and so on. As a result, the airline started an experimental program that placed cabin attendant trainees in the classroom for a certain period and then gave them additional training during an evaluation training flight. On these flights, experienced cabin attendants provided the trainees with S-OJT based on a list of job tasks. Some tasks, such as serving meals and snacks, were demonstrated during the actual delivery of services to passengers. Other tasks were presented away from passengers during the relatively free periods between meal services.

The coal extraction division of American Electric Power uses S-OJT as part of its broad safety training programs. Safety training conducted in the classroom focuses primarily on the rules and regulations related to safe work practices and in the handling of hazardous materials. In the work setting, task trainers train each employee, managers and hourly employees alike, on specific tasks related to safety in their immediate work area. The results suggest that training that addresses different training objectives in different training locations improves safety outcomes. In one coal mine, training reduced the number of lost days caused by back injuries.

The Kuwait National Petroleum Company uses structured on-the-job training as the primary training approach to develop newly hired engineering graduates in the refinery operations. The engineer-trainees follow a prescribed set of tasks, which often take over one year to complete. Classroom training programs are used in combination with the structured on-the-job training to address the many prerequisite areas of knowledge and skill required of engineers. The trainers are responsible for identifying the areas of need, and the HRD department coordinates the offering of these common training programs.

S-OJT AND COMMUNICATIONS TECHNOLOGY

The use of communications technology along with S-OJT is an emerging and promising opportunity for organizations. Indeed, the use of communications technology seems a growing necessity for S-OJT, not a nice-to-have option. Some form of communications technology might be used to support any one of the four basic ways of using S-OJT that have been described. Communications technology are the devices used to store, send, and receive information about the training. Experience has shown three related uses of communications technology for S-OJT: document management systems, trainer–trainee interactions, and learning networks.

Document Management Systems

One of the most critical issues in S-OJT is ensuring that trainers use the most up-to-date versions of the training modules. Unfortunately, in many organizations, more than one version is being used by trainers at the same time, much to the concern of managers. Having a document management system makes the most recent sets of training materials accessible for revising and training. In general, document management systems are becoming more common in organizations. However, to be useful for S-OJT, such systems need to be dynamic in that they allow access for those involved in revising the documents and for those in need of accessing the documents. For example, HRD staff should be able to review the documents online and make any changes necessary to improve the documents, trainers should be able to download the trainer's version of the training module, and trainees should be able to download the trainee's version of the training module.

A growing number of organizations are at the initial stages of implementing a document management system for the training materials used with S-OJT. Part of the issue is simply the volume of documents that are to be used by trainers across many locations. A large Asian airline is now in the process of identifying all S-OJT training materials related to reservations, ticketing, and airport services, with the intent of ensuring that they have a standard format of presenting them and making them accessible by trainers on a worldwide basis.

Trainer–Trainee Interactions

It is intriguing to consider the possible changes in trainer–trainee interactions when using communications technology. Until recently, S-OJT assumed that the trainer and trainee would be physically next to each other. That arrangement defines much of the uniqueness of OJT compared to other training approaches. Given the demands of new work situations and dispersion of individuals across global organizations, however, close trainer–trainee proximity cannot be possible in all training situations.

Consider the growing number of situations in which employees work alone on-site at the customer's location. This is the case of customer engineers with Liebert Global Services (LGS), an organization that provides maintenance services for precision power backup and air-conditioning systems for client organizations. LGS offers maintenance services on its own products and its competitors. As a result, in the course of a workday, customer engineers might encounter a wide range of products to be inspected and serviced. Communications technology would allow access to a virtual library of training documents, both internal LGS documents and external documents available from other manufacturers. Such information could be retrieved through the employees' wireless modems installed on their laptop computers.

In a traditional sense, the trainer could be alongside the customer engineers to perform the S-OJT. However, it is more often the case that the trainer cannot possibly be at the trainee's location. Similar to many organizations, LGS has operations worldwide and a limited number of experienced employees available for training. Thus, S-OJT trainers could be stationed at a central corporate location, available for training on call. The trainer-by-distance could be available to interact live with the trainee through an Internet connection or cellular phone hookup. Together, they would be able to review the same documents online—and possibly with the use of digital cameras to send and receive data—each of them would be able to view the same work situation as well.

Learning Networks

Finally, communications technology could be useful as part of learning networks. Several authors have described how organizations have used networked work teams—that is, individuals participating as team members to solve problems, make decisions, and discuss policy from remote locations. In some organizations, such as Hewlett-Packard, networked teams have become melded parts of the corporate culture (Shockley-Zalabak & Buffington Burmeister, 2001).

In the same way, learning networks would be used to connect individuals at different locations for the purpose of exchanging training information or generating training information that does not currently exist. In this sense, the notion of a person being a subject-matter expert is becoming an increasingly fluid concept. No one individual seems to have all information necessary about a topic, making it necessary at times to use collective understandings as the basis for the training content. Indeed, trainees themselves may have information to contribute, which makes a learning network all the more desirable arrangement.

SELECTION FACTORS

Organizations use S-OJT in a variety of ways. The question remains: Under what conditions should it be used? As stated, S-OJT—and any type of training for that matter—should be used only when analysis shows that employees are not performing as required because they lack the appropriate level of competence to do so. This is the principal condition for taking such action. The point is that an informed decision should be made each time S-OJT is considered for use.

Five selection factors determine whether S-OJT is appropriate for a given training situation:

- the nature of the work,
- the resources available,
- constraints in the work setting,
- financial considerations, and
- individual differences.

In practice, the selection factors should be used in connection with an inventory listing the units of work that employees should learn. Each unit on the inventory should be matched with the selection factors to determine whether structured OJT is suitable for it.

Nature of the Work

The first selection factor concerns the nature of the task. Four issues are related to the nature of the work: immediacy, frequency, difficulty, and consequences of error.

Immediacy

Do employees require the work information right now, or can they receive it later on without hurting production or service delivery? Managers often consider immediacy to be the most crucial issue. At times, the best approach may be to dispense information by bringing groups together off the job. S-OJT can be suitable when logistical or scheduling problems prevent individuals from being together as a group.

Frequency

Frequency involves the number of times an employee performs the work during a given work period. Some units of work, such as giving performance feedback to subordinates or maintaining equipment, can be performed only once or twice per year. Other work can be repeated many times during a single workday. S-OJT may be easier to schedule when the work is done often.

Difficulty

Work difficulty should be thought of in terms not only of inherent difficulty but also of employees' abilities. Some work can be difficult simply because employees lack the prerequisites to perform the work. Other employees may find them easier. Nevertheless, S-OJT can be more suitable for difficult work because it makes the information more concrete. S-OJT may not be suitable for work that involves speed of performance or safety hazards. And some low-difficulty tasks might be acquired through the use of job performance guides alone.

Consequences of Error

The consequences of error in the performance of the work should also be considered. What are the consequences to the organization or to the individuals if the work is not done correctly? The consequences can be represented by lost customers, reduced profits, destroyed property, psychological harm, or physical injury. S-OJT may be more suitable when the consequences of error are high and difficulty is low. When the consequences of error and difficulty are both high, S-OJT may be less suitable. Work where the difficulty is high can be learned with the aid of simulators or in off-the-job practice areas. These settings allow and can even encourage employees to make errors so that they can view the results of error firsthand without doing permanent harm.

Available Resources

The second selection factor is the resources available in the work setting that can be used in the training. S-OJT requires that trainees be able to do something or know something at the end of the training session. For such outcomes to be achieved, the various resources required for the training should be available in the work setting. Otherwise, the impact of the training will be lessened. Three sets of resources must be considered: people; time for training; and equipment, tools, or data.

People
People deliver S-OJT, and they are sometimes needed to support it. Above all, S-OJT requires experienced employees, who conduct the training. The organization may not have employees who are experts in a given unit of work. This situation often occurs when a new piece of equipment or technology is brought in and no one on-site has had time to develop sufficient levels of competence. In such cases, selected employees must either be sent away to an off-site training program or be given time to develop the competence on their own. Then, they can use S-OJT to train others.

Time for Training

The next crucial question is whether there is adequate time for training during the workday. Managers are often reluctant to take way their best performers, even for short periods of time. Managers have been heard to say, "We are too busy"; "We can't stop production to train people in this way"; or "It sounds nice to have the OJT structured and all, but it seems better suited for companies that don't have our tight schedules."

Attempting to squeeze in both work and S-OJT into the same work schedule is generally not productive. The quality of both the work and the training suffers. Whenever work time and training time have to compete, work usually wins. In some instances, S-OJT is conducted at times other than regular work hours, such as before work, during breaks, or after the workday.

Equipment, Tools, and Data

When S-OJT trains employees how to use equipment, tools, or data, these resources must be made available in the work setting. Making them available can pose logistical problems. A busy organization generally cannot take a piece of production equipment out of service just for training purposes. Alternate ways should be found when work schedules are tight. For instance, Eddie Bauer, Inc., has designated training areas on the warehouse floor at which S-OJT is delivered to newly hired warehouse employees. If the proper equipment, tools, or data cannot be provided in the work setting, then S-OJT is probably not suitable.

Constraints in Work Setting

To some extent, any work setting is an inconvenient place in which to conduct training; thus, virtually all work settings have constraints. Flexibility and creativity are often required to make certain that training does not become a burden for managers and employees. Two constraints must always be considered: training location and work distractions.

Training Location

Here are some suitable locations for S-OJT: an office, a retail sales floor, training station within the production area, a conference room, a computer station, a work bench, an assembly line, an observation booth, a lunch room, a nuclear power control room simulator, or even the passenger cabin of a commercial airliner. As described, training staff at KLM Royal Dutch Airlines report that S-OJT is being conducted for flight attendants during the flight and even in front of passengers. Follow-up has shown that training has no effect on service quality and that passengers generally appreciate seeing the training take place.

S-OJT has even been conducted in an automobile, since this was the most appropriate place for a newly hired cable salesperson to be trained by an experienced salesperson as the two traveled between client locations. The training location selected essentially depends on what training resources are necessary to achieve the training objectives.

A number of constraints in the work setting can affect the suitability of training locations. For instance, S-OJT could not be conducted when both the experienced employee and the trainee were wearing protective bodysuits and oxygen masks in a spray paint booth. In this case, the training was conducted outside the spray booth before the gear was put on. However, S-OJT is being conducted in clean room conditions in a hard-disk manufacturer in Singapore, even though both the trainer and trainee are wearing full bodysuits. The necessity of being able to inspect the hard disks during the process makes it necessary that the training occur in that location.

It would also be inappropriate to conduct S-OJT in circumstances that could embarrass the trainee in front of customers or other employees. If a suitable training location cannot be found, S-OJT is probably not suitable.

Work Distractions

Does the work setting have inherent distractions or performance demands that could inhibit learning, induce stress, or place the trainee in physical or psychological jeopardy? Work distractions often include ambient noise, safety hazards, background activity, work schedules, or onlookers. When such distractions are conspicuous, they will lessen the effectiveness of any training provided, and they can even lead to unintended violations of safety rules. It is extremely important for training to follow all safety precautions.

Most work settings contain sufficient distractions to make S-OJT difficult to conduct without taking some preliminary measures. However, only a few environments, such as nuclear power plants or air traffic control towers, are totally inappropriate for training. Learning new information can be stressful enough in itself, and the additional pressure of relocating during training can take a toll on trainees and trainers alike.

Financial Considerations

S-OJT has financial considerations that should be taken into account. At the same time, it is wise to view the costs of S-OJT or any structured training program as an investment from which the organization can expect a return. A decision based on costs alone can be unwise. Two financial elements are important: the number of trainees and the predicted financial benefits.

Number of Trainees

Mangum (1985) has suggested that the suitability of OJT decreases as the number of trainees increases, since the costs associated with off-site training programs can be spread out over more individuals. This assessment is accurate only to the extent that the total number of people trained is distinguished from the number of people who need training at any one time. S-OJT is appropriate when the number of people who need training at a given time is low, even though the total number of people trained overall is high. Off-the-job training approaches make sense only when large numbers of employees need training at one time. The financial forecasting model described in the next section helps compare these situations.

Predicted Financial Benefits

Logically, an organization would consider the best deal to be the training approach predicted to provide the most financial benefits at the lowest cost. Until recently, information of this nature was perceived to be useful but hard to obtain. Swanson (2001) reports a method of comparing the financial benefits that can forecast the benefits of various HRD program options. The method proposes that each program option has a performance value and the benefit equals performance value minus cost.

All other things being equal, S-OJT should be selected only if performance value exceeds costs. Studies show that the costs of S-OJT are higher than those of unstructured OJT but that the additional costs resulted in greater financial benefits for the organization (Jacobs et al., 1992). Thus, cost figures alone cannot be used to determine the suitability of S-OJT. It is more prudent to consider all aspects of the equation. S-OJT can cost more, say, than a classroom training course, but it may also provide more financial benefits, since it trains employees more efficiently. In the end, use of a job performance guide would be more financially beneficial for the organization.

Individual Differences

The individual differences among trainees are the last major factor. While people are alike in many ways, they also differ in ways that can affect the success of a training program. The concern here is whether trainees differ in ways that might hinder the effectiveness of S-OJT. Experiences suggests that S-OJT affects individual trainees in different ways. Some trainees behave as they would in any other training situation. Others become anxious and withdrawn. A few become more defensive about their abilities. Three individual differences deserve consideration: trainee prerequisites, trainee preferences, and cultural differences.

Trainee Prerequisites

Regardless of the approach used, training is always more effective when trainees possess the prerequisite knowledge, skills, and readiness. Prerequisite knowledge and skills include technical background, comfort with the use of tools and equipment, literacy, and previous work experiences. Trainees must also be ready to learn the information. That is, they must anticipate learning the information without undue anxiety or resistance. Of course, trainees should enter a training session with enthusiasm and interest.

Having the proper prerequisites seems especially critical when determining whether to use S-OJT. S-OJT is not appropriate for conveying information that trainees should have learned or for arousing interest in a topic that the trainee finds irrelevant. Some of these issues can be addressed by the way the training is conducted. However, if critical trainee prerequisites are not present, then S-OJT may not be suitable.

Trainee Preferences

Research has shown that some persons learn more simply because the instructional approach has been consistent with their preferred styles of learning, which are based on some personality variables (Cronbach & Snow, 1977). Thus, it is appropriate to consider personality differences when deciding whether to use S-OJT. For example, field-dependent persons—that is, people who have difficulty perceiving simple figures within a complex field—have more difficulty than field-independent persons in identifying the critical features of concepts, and they ask more questions related to the instruction.

While no studies have investigated the relationship between S-OJT and trainee preferences, the results of other studies suggest that they are related. On occasion, some trainees react better to S-OJT than others, no matter what the content or the trainee's ability to learn the task. Preferences for or against the use of S-OJT may be based on reactions to the relative degree of rigidity that it imposes on the instructional condition.

Cultural Differences

Another basis for trainee preferences comes from the cultures of trainees and trainers (Osman-Gani, 2001). Few organizations exist in which the trainer and trainee have the same national origins, and this observation is true in both U.S. and international organizations. For example, the state of Ohio has many manufacturing and production organizations in which senior managers and engineers are Japanese expatriates, while most front-line employees are Americans. In Singapore, many managers in the high-tech sector are ethnic Chinese, who supervise guest workers from Malaysia, southern India, or Bangladesh. Chapter 12 discusses how national culture might influence behavior and the instructional consequences of these differing behaviors.

Table 4.1 summarizes the selection factors discussed here that can help you to decide whether to use S-OJT, also providing space for comments regarding each factor. In practice, some selection factors may be more relevant than others, and some may not apply at all. Moreover, a final decision is often influenced by subjective factors that the checklist does not account for, such as the preferences of management and the organization's commitment to training.

TABLE 4.1. S-OJT Selection Factors

Unit of Work: _____

APPROPRIATENESS OF FACTOR (✓)

Factor	Comments
_____ Nature of the work ■ Immediacy ■ Frequency ■ Difficulty ■ Consequences of error	_____
_____ Resources available ■ People ■ Time for training ■ Equipment, tools, data	_____
_____ Constraints in work setting ■ Training location ■ Work distractions	_____
_____ Financial considerations ■ Number of trainees ■ Predicted financial benefits	_____
_____ Individual differences ■ Trainee prerequisites ■ Trainee preferences ■ Cultural differences	_____

Final selection decision: _____

Clearly, these considerations also should be taken into account. Thus, professional judgment plays a part in making sound selection decisions.

CONCLUSION

Although S-OJT has been shown to be effective in many different training situations, it is not appropriate in every situation. An informed decision should be made each time it is considered for use. If S-OJT is selected, the next step of the process calls for the analysis of the unit of work.

Chapter 5
Analyzing the Work to Be Learned

Once the decision to use S-OJT has been made, the next step of the process is to analyze the work that should be learned. This chapter examines the following topics:

- What is meant by units of work
- How to plan the work analysis
- Using the work analysis information

UNITS OF WORK WITHIN JOBS

S-OJT is not meant to train employees how to do an entire job. Rather, it focuses on relatively small units of related work information. In some situations, these units of work are referred to as *tasks*. The term *work* is used instead of *task* because of the wide range of situations in which S-OJT can be used. Not all S-OJT situations involve the learning of tasks per se. Rather, some S-OJT situations involve learning how to complete projects, special assignments, or some other set of work that cannot be adequately defined as a task in a traditional sense. Regardless of the term used, the emphasis of

S-OJT remains on specific components of jobs and not on entire jobs.

Many other training approaches share this same emphasis. However, emphasizing specific units of work is even more pronounced for S-OJT than it is for these other approaches. Most off-the-job training programs address several units of work or broad topics of information, perhaps to make the time spent away from the job seem worthwhile. In contrast, S-OJT focuses only on a strictly limited set of related work at a time.

The notion that work is composed of specific units is associated with traditional understandings of technical-skilled work. That is, jobs have units of work that are mutually exclusive from other units of work. This understanding about the nature of jobs remains central even in the flexible work environments of the global economy. As the boundaries between jobs have become less distinct, units of work have become the focus. Jobs are less isolated from one another today, so that each unit of work is not necessarily a small operation that has limited meaning but an effort that results in a performance outcome. Thus, jobs are likely to have more diversity and complexity (Swanson, 2002).

Units of work have two basic components: a set of well-defined behaviors and the performance outcomes that result from the behaviors.

Consider when individuals are called upon to troubleshoot customer service problems, an activity found in many organizations with a strong customer orientation. This unit of work has both a behavioral component—troubleshooting the customer's problems—and an outcome component—the result must meet the organization's specification for interacting with customers.

Work Behaviors

Work behaviors are the thoughts, actions, and decisions necessary that one must make to perform the work. Behaviors are often at the most detailed level of analysis used to describe work. Since units of work can differ widely in their content, each is analyzed into different types of behaviors. For example, installing a replacement part on a piece of equipment requires the employee to perform a series of steps in a specified order. However, identifying which part was faulty involves a completely different set of behaviors: matching the symptoms of the problem with its likely causes and taking the actions required to solve the problem. While the two units of work—troubleshooting the problem and installing the replacement part—are highly interdependent, it is justified to consider them to be distinct because each unit of work places differing behavioral demands on the person who performs it.

While work behaviors differ, they tend to differ in fairly consistent patterns. Regardless of the job, most jobs are composed of work that requires problems to be solved, work that requires decisions to be made, work that requires inspections to be done, work that requires a set of sequential steps to be performed, and so on.

Table 5.1 describes nine characteristic behavioral patterns commonly found when analyzing work. Some work can contain more than one behavioral pattern, as when performing a procedure requires a decision to be made or a problem to be solved. Workflows are included as a behavioral pattern even though they are performed by more than one individual. Individuals still require an understanding of this behavioral pattern.

The behavioral patterns associated with particular units of work are usually related to job titles. For example, management and supervisory jobs are likely to have units of work involving the behaviors of planning and organizing resources that affect others, while skilled technical jobs are likely to have units of work involving behaviors that make use of tools or equipment. Today's work expectations have created many exceptions to this rule. That is, many skilled

TABLE 5.1. Patterns of Work Behavior		
Behavior	*Description*	*Information to Document*
PROCEDURE	Performing a series of steps in a specific order	■ Steps of the procedure ■ Quality requirements ■ Safety information ■ Embedded decisions and troubleshooting components
TROUBLE-SHOOTING	Matching existing problem situations or indicators with probable causes and the actions that are likely to resolve them	■ Problem situations or indicators ■ Probable causes of each problem ■ Actions to take for each cause
DECISION MAKING	Determining the action to take based on the arrangement of varying conditions in a given situation	■ Conditions that vary ■ Decisions related to combinations of conditions
INSPECTING	Determining the accuracy of the match between a given product or process and a model	■ Inspection points ■ Steps to inspect each point ■ Criteria overall and for each point
ADJUSTING/REVISING	Improving a product or process in order to meet a standard	■ Areas or points to adjust/revise ■ Effects of making the adjustment or revision ■ Steps to make the adjustment or revision ■ Examples

TABLE 5.1. *(continued)*

Behavior	Description	Information to Document
PLANNING	Gathering information and performing coordinated actions to achieve a goal	■ Information to gather ■ Resources to use ■ Process steps ■ Techniques and tools to make the plan ■ Goals to achieve
CALCULATING	Doing a set of operations to determine a value	■ Required sets of information ■ Steps in the calculation ■ Consequences of each step ■ Meaning of the results ■ Examples
WORKFLOW	Recognizing the series of actions over time that convert inputs into outputs	■ Action steps ■ Decisions ■ Troubleshooting ■ Inspection ■ Auto inputs
COMPRE-HENDING	Recognizing an instance of a class of ideas, actions, or things	■ Operational definition ■ Critical attributes ■ Variable attributes ■ Positive and negative examples

technical employees use tools as part of their jobs, while many managers are involved in the planning and organizing of work. Nevertheless, the ability to see and anticipate discrete patterns of work behaviors, regardless of the job involved, is an important aspect of understanding work.

Performance Outcomes

Work also has performance outcomes. Performance outcomes describe the results to which the behaviors lead. Performance outcomes can be stated in terms of the *quantity* of the products produced or services rendered or *quality* of the products or services provided. *Quantity* outcomes involve:

- volume—the number completed;
- rate—the number completed over a period of time;
- schedule—the timeliness in meeting a deadline; and
- productivity ratios—the outputs divided into the inputs.

Quality outcomes involve:

- accuracy—the match between a model and a sample;
- class—the perceived features of a product or service; and
- novelty—the perceived extraordinary nature of a product or service.

Performance outcomes help determine the adequacy of the work behaviors. If the desired performance outcomes are not attained, then the cause may lie in the behaviors of the persons performing the task. One cannot judge the adequacy of the work behaviors without first examining the performance outcomes that result from those behaviors. This is the essence of the performance analysis process.

Work statements are used to capture the information about work behaviors and the associated performance outcomes. In S-OJT, work statements are used to communicate the training content and outcomes to trainers and trainees. They help us clarify the boundaries of the unit of work relative to other units of work. A work statement has two elements: an action verb and an object noun. The action verb describes what the person does, and the object noun describes what the person acts upon or what his or her action affects. Here are some typical statements that describe units of work from a variety of professional, skilled technical, and management and supervisory positions:

- Calculate interest and principal payments on consumer mortgage loans.
- Troubleshoot customer service problems.
- Determine insurance deductibles based on customer needs.
- Install replacement dies in metal-stamping machine.
- Present a rationale for financial planning to individuals who request retirement information.
- Facilitate root-cause analysis team meetings.

Each of these units of work represents a distinct set of behaviors and distinct performance outcomes. Most jobs are made up of many units of work. The ability of an experienced employee to perform a particular unit of work depends on his or her understanding of and ability to carry out the behaviors that make up the work. For someone else to be able to learn the same behaviors and achieve the same performance outcomes in the most efficient and effective way possible, the component parts must be analyzed and then organized in ways that facilitate learning. This is the basic purpose of work analysis.

PLANNING WORK ANALYSIS FOR S-OJT

Work analysis is the process of making explicit the behaviors, performance outcomes, prerequisite knowledge, skills, attitudes, and other relevant information to a unit of work. This information is used to prepare the S-OJT module that corresponds to the unit of work. Because work analysis provides such a wealth of information, it is one of the most critical steps of the S-OJT process.

Work analysis seeks to find the best way of performing a unit of work while recognizing that "best" is a relative notion. In practice, disagreements can arise over how some work is presently done. The work will change as improvements are made. Work analysis is used to capture what is best for the organization at a particular moment. In this sense, work analysis seeks to show those who must perform the work how to complete it without risk of physical or psychological harm, in the shortest amount of time and the least amount of effort, and at the lowest cost.

Work analysis is usually conducted as an iterative activity in which work information is gathered and draft documents are prepared, reviewed by experts and stakeholders, and revised as their comments suggest. Often, the cycle just described is repeated several times before the analysis is complete.

You can plan a work analysis for S-OJT by constructing a matrix that matches information sources with data-gathering methods for each of the major products covered by the work analysis. For example, Table 5.2 presents the plan for analyzing the sample task, troubleshooting customer service problems. The table shows how to plan to gather information about work behaviors. Information is gathered about performance outcomes by reviewing performance appraisal documents and by interviewing experienced employees' supervisors. Information is obtained about customer requirements and quality by reviewing existing training materials, reviewing company standards, and interviewing experts.

As Table 5.2 suggests, each product covered by the work analysis may require a different source of information and a different method of gathering the information. Your selection of sources and methods should be based on the purpose of the analysis, nature of the work, the accessibility of experts, and time constraints and other organizational fac-

TABLE 5.2. Work Analysis Plan			
Unit of Work: Troubleshooting customer service problems			
INFORMATION SOURCES/DATA-GATHERING METHODS			
Analyze existing documents: work analysis reports, standard operating procedures, training manuals, customer requirements, internal quality standards, and safety documents.	Observe experts as they perform the work.	Interview experts about the work.	Ask experts to respond to questionnaires about the work.
PRODUCTS			
WORK BEHAVIORS	✓	✓	
PERFORMANCE OUTCOMES ✓		✓	
PREREQUISITES ✓		✓	
RESOURCES ✓	✓		
SAFETY/ QUALITY INFORMATION ✓		✓	

tors. Several resources are recommended to help match sources and methods, such as Swanson (2002); Jonassen, Hannum, and Tessmer (1989); and Zemke and Kramlinger (1984). Most authorities recommend that you use as many different sources and methods as possible, since it helps reduce the kind of systematic error that can result from the use of any one source or method alone.

Products of Work Analysis

A work analysis typically has five major products: work behaviors, performance outcomes, prerequisites, resources, and additional information about safety and quality.

Work Behaviors
The goal of work analysis is to identify the exact nature of the behaviors required to do a unit of work. In identifying them, it also reveals the relationships between them. For example, for a procedural task, it determines which step comes first, which comes second, and so on. The underlying pattern emerges when the behaviors are viewed together: procedure, decision making, problem solving, inspection, concept, and principle, among others. These behaviors form the content of the S-OJT program.

Performance Outcomes
Work analysis also seeks to make explicit the performance outcomes that result from the behaviors. As noted, performance outcomes can be stated in terms of the quantity or quality of the products or services that result from performing the unit of work.

Prerequisites
In the process of analyzing the work behaviors, the prerequisite areas of knowledge, skills, and attitudes are identified. Successful performance of a unit of work requires the employees who perform it to possess the necessary prerequisites.

Resources
Work task analysis also identifies the resources required to do the work, including specialized tools, equipment, data, people, and time. Listing these resources can also reveal more general areas of prerequisite knowledge and skills,

such as basic knowledge of tool usage, math and reading skills, computer literacy, or blueprint reading, to name only a few.

Additional Work Information

Additional work information can include quality requirements, safety precautions, or special hazards or difficulty—any information pertaining to the work that might be useful when the S-OJT module is prepared.

Information Sources

The sources of information for a work analysis can basically be separated into two major categories: documents and people.

Documents

Organizations typically have an array of documents that describe how a task has been done in the past and how it should be done in the future. These documents can include previous work analysis reports, standard operating procedures, manufacturer's manuals, technical manuals, customer information, and safety specifications. Documents are especially useful when the work represents a totally new area of information in the organization, as it does when new technology is introduced, and when the number of experienced employees is small.

People

The people who can provide information required for the work analysis can be experienced employees, job incumbents, supervisors, safety specialists, engineers, union officials, and representatives from external suppliers.

Gathering information from these individuals can sometimes be difficult, simply because of the nature of experts.

Beyond possessing more knowledge and skill than their peer in some specific domain, experts have unique ways of thinking and using information that differ sharply from those of most others around them (Chi et al., 1988).

These differences sometimes make it difficult for them to communicate information about some unit of work. Extensive experience with expert employees led to the following observations:

- Experts always seem to demonstrate or explain their work behaviors quickly and with a great deal of ease.

- Experts have rarely given much thought to their actions before you ask them, and their work behaviors have in many instances become automatic.

- Experts usually believe that most of what they do is easy, and they cannot understand why others have difficulty attaining the same level of expertise.

- Several experts who perform the same unit of work usually each have their own way of doing the work, although the essential aspects of how each performs the work is similar in most respects, and the performance outcomes are the same as well.

- Experts often say one thing and do another, primarily because they are not totally aware of all the things they do.

Thus, to gather accurate and complete information, experienced employees should be carefully observed to make certain that what they say and do are consistent.

Information-Gathering Methods

There are four methods of gathering work task analysis information: observation, interviews, questionnaires, and content analysis.

Observation
Observation helps make even the most subtle work behaviors explicit. Experts do not always realize that they are doing something and thus do not report it. Observation helps us fill in the gaps that result.

Interviews
Talking to experts in different venues is another way of gathering work information. Formal interviews can be conducted individually, in small groups, or as part of group process activities such as using a focus group, nominal group technique, and DACUM (developing a curriculum), among others.

Questionnaires
Giving experts an inventory of the units of work and asking them to react is probably the most frequently used way of gathering work information. Questionnaires allow large numbers of people to supply information about specific aspects of the work, such as difficulty, frequency, and training requirements.

Content Analysis
Synthesizing the information culled from documents and other printed resources into outlines, graphs, and tables is another method of gathering work information.

To conclude, considering the sources and methods appropriate for each product of the work analysis helps make a plan for the work analysis. But one must never view a plan as being unalterable. Unanticipated issues and constraints can often arise. For instance, particular experienced employees can be called away from their jobs. In such cases, you will have to rely on other people for information and perhaps also on documents.

USING THE WORK ANALYSIS INFORMATION

Once you have completed the work analysis, you need to make the information useful for the preparation of S-OJT modules. This usually involves three basic activities: specifying training objectives, organizing work behaviors for learning purposes, and developing performance tests to accompany the training.

Specify Training Objectives

Training objectives are statements that describe the behavior expected of the trainee at the conclusion of S-OJT. They are derived from performance outcomes, which are identified as part of the work analysis. According to Mager (1999), training objectives have three components: the *conditions* under which the trainee demonstrates his or her ability to do the work, including such things as the use of resources, constraints, setting; the *behaviors* that the trainee must demonstrate when performing the work; and the *standards* by which the learned behavior is judged—time, accuracy, and quantity.

In most instances, the standards component differs from the levels expected from work outcomes. Trainees are not likely to achieve the same levels when they begin to learn the work and when they have experience in doing it later on. Thus, the standards component of training objectives should accommodate the abilities of trainees who do not have the benefit of experience or prolonged practice.

Organize Work Behaviors

Work behaviors must be organized in a way that makes them easy to learn. Often, this means representing the work in a way that seems totally different from the way the work is actually accomplished. Consider that the way in which conceptual information is organized can bear little resemblance to the way in which the information is used in the work setting. Describing an operational definition, specifying critical and variable attributes, and developing positive and negative examples are all part of analyzing conceptual information. The hierarchical analysis technique (Gagne, Briggs, & Wager, 1988) can be used to organize related sets of conceptual information.

Some other work-related information, such as problem solving and decision making, may appear to be linear activities. In fact, problem-solving behaviors usually look like a table of information that matches problem situations with causes and actions. For instance, Table 5.3 shows one page of how the inspection of a manufactured part was documented for S-OJT. The first column of the document shows two of the inspection points, the middle column shows the steps to accomplish each of the inspection points, and the right column shows the criteria related to the inspection points.

Table 5.4 shows one page of how troubleshooting an industrial robot was documented for S-OJT. The first column shows the problem indicator, the middle column shows the cause of the problem, and the right column shows the actions to correct the problem.

Figure 5.1 shows a page from a S-OJT module for direct sales representatives showing their sales order process, which is an example of a workflow pattern. Other units of behavior require different approaches. Decision making is usually organized by matching the varying conditions with different actions.

At this point, any additional work-related information that was generated from the work analysis should be included. As noted, the additional information can include such issues as safety and quality. Often, the additional information can be represented in the form of visuals (e.g., photographs, illustrations, or drawings).

TABLE 5.3. Work Document of an Inspection

Inspection Point	Procedure	Criteria
PART/NET SURFACE FLUSH	1. Place flush block X on net surface with pin in bushing hole. NOTE: Flush block X is only used with part 20561427. 2. Place LO edge of flush template A on part and NET edge on net surface. 3. Slide flush template A around part. NOTE: At finger lift place NET edge on flush block X (part 20561427 only). 4. Place HI edge of flush template A on part and NET edge on net surface. 5. Slide flush template A around part. NOTE: At finger lift place NET edge on flush block X (part 20561427 only).	■ LO edge of flush part template A touches all around. ■ HI edge of flush template A **does not** touch part.
PART EDGE/NET BLOCK CLEARANCE	1. Place feeler gauge between part edge and net block, then slide around outer edge.	■ GO portion of feeler gauge fits between net block and part. ■ No GO portion of feeler gauge **does not** fit between net block and part.

TABLE 5.4. Work Document of Troubleshooting		
Problem	*Likely Cause*	*Action*
592 User Message Alarm	Address check did not confirm actual robot position.	Use the following to restart the line: 1. Identify the alarm location. 2. Lock out the robot. 3. Press "Shift Up" then "Reset" button in sequence to clear alarm. 4. Compare address checkpoint with actual robot position when alarm occurred. 5. Determine action based on table below: If address check and robot position DON'T MATCH, 1. Inspect robot for disconnected air lines, electrical wires, or other apparent problems. 2. If no apparent problems found, call electrician. If address check and robot position MATCH, 1. Call electrician.

Develop Performance Tests

Performance tests can also be developed at this time. Most S-OJT makes use of tests that measure a trainee's ability to do something, not just to know something. For that reason, most tests that accompany S-OJT are in the form of performance rating scales.

The trainer uses performance-rating scales at the end of training. Two different types of performance-rating scales are used when predetermined standards are available:

Sales Order Flow

?

What would happen if DSRs were unaware of the sales workflow?

- How would it affect our customers?
- How would it affect your compensation?

The specific steps of the sales workflow might differ at various locations. The following shows steps common to all offices.

Sales Order Flow

1. DSR completes sales order with customer.
2. DSR forwards sales order to sales administrator.
3. Sales administrator inspects sales order to:
   - confirm order accuracy;
   - determine if it is a serviceable address;
   - conduct customer credit check, if necessary;
   - record installation instructions.
4. Sales administrator provides receipt to DSR for cash received from customer.
5. Sales administrator forwards sales order to customer service representative.
6. Customer service representative initiates/restarts customer account.
7. Telemarketing representative (or auto caller) contacts customer confirming next day installation.
8. Installation supervisor forwards order to installer.
9. Installer installs service in customer's home.
10. Customer signs installation order and agreement accepting responsibility for equipment.
11. Installer forwards installation order and customer agreement to customer service representative.
12. Customer service representative enters completed order into system.
13. System logs compensation percentage in DSR account.

Figure 5.1. Training Manual Showing a Workflow

- Checklist—this type of rating scale is used by trainers to rate a trainee's use of a process.

- Product—this type of rating scale is used by trainers to rate the outcomes that a trainee achieves in using the process.

```
Unit of Work: _____

A. Data-gathering methods    _____

B. Information sources        _____

C. Training objective
     ▪ Performance condition   _____
     ▪ Work behavior           _____
     ▪ Standard             Time: _____
                            Accuracy: _____
                            Quantity: _____

D. Work patterns              _____
                              _____
                              _____

E. Type of performance test   _____
                              _____
                              _____
```

Figure 5.2. Work Analysis Summary Sheet

For example, judging the adequacy of a sales plan calls for a product scale, while judging the adequacy of the planning behaviors that went into preparing the sales plan calls for a process scale. Additional information about developing different types of performance tests can be obtained from Shrock and Coscarelli (1989) and Westgaard (1993).

Figure 5.2 presents a summary sheet that helps ensure that a work analysis has been planned adequately and that the resulting work analysis information is ready for use in preparing the S-OJT module. Chapter 7 describes the preparation of S-OJT modules.

CONCLUSION

Once the decision has been made to use S-OJT, the units of work to be learned must be analyzed in depth. S-OJT focuses on the work unit level, or on small sets of job information. Units of work represent the behaviors and their performance outcomes. Work analysis is the process of identifying the component parts of units of work and gathering relevant information about them. The resulting work analysis information is used to prepare the S-OJT modules.

Chapter 6

Selecting, Training, and Managing Employees to Deliver Structured On-the-Job Training

The question of who should deliver S-OJT tends to arise early in the process. Should the delivery of S-OJT be limited to certain employees only, such as supervisors and selected front-line employees? Or should all experienced employees be expected to conduct S-OJT? These questions should be addressed before the organization uses S-OJT. This chapter answers three questions:

- What are the basic requirements for S-OJT trainers?
- How do you select, train, and manage S-OJT trainers?
- Is there a need to certify S-OJT trainers?

BASIC S-OJT TRAINER REQUIREMENTS

In its most basic form, S-OJT involves having an experienced employee or trainer present work-related information to another employee one-on-one. However, S-OJT means more than just having Julia teach Joe how to do her job (Kondrasuk, 1979). S-OJT trainers should have basic requirements in two areas: They should have adequate competence in the unit of work that comprises the content of the training, and they should have adequate competence as a trainer.

If trainers do not meet the requirements in both areas, the effectiveness and efficiency of the training are likely at risk. However well the other steps of the S-OJT process have been performed, much of the success of S-OJT—or any training program, for that matter—depends on the trainer's having the right skills (Johnson & Leach, 2001; Powers, 1992). This view does not mean that the number of employees whom you can involve as trainers is limited. Indeed, many more employees than what might be expected can be involved as S-OJT trainers. The issue is one of using the right employees in each situation.

SELECTING, TRAINING, AND MANAGING TRAINERS

Traditionally, those who have delivered OJT have been supervisors or certain front-line employees, such as lead persons, who are recognized as experts. This expectation continues in many organizations today (Broadwell, 1986). Yet in reality, few trainers ever receive sufficient preparation, although this situation has begun to change. Increasing numbers of companies are recognizing that they need to select and train their S-OJT trainers in a more comprehensive and formal way.

Nevertheless, in most instances, few trainers receive more than a single program on coaching or one-on-one training techniques. This isolated training experience is rarely enough to ensure that the training will be reliable (Johnson & Leach, 2001; Wichman, 1989). At best, existing programs offer an overview of one small part of the process—delivering the content. At worst, these programs mislead managers into believing that such experience is all that trainer development requires.

Developing experienced employees to be S-OJT trainers, whether they are managers, supervisors, or experienced front-line employees, is a process unto itself. The development process has four steps: (1) identify selection criteria, (2) select the trainers, (3) train the trainers, and, (4) manage trainer performance.

Identifying Selection Criteria

Each unit of work imposes its own set of trainer selection criteria. Nevertheless, every S-OJT trainer requires some measure of the following qualities:

- *Adequate competence in the work.* Adequate competence in the work involves the documented ability to perform the work behaviors and achieve the performance outcomes at a level that consistently meets or exceeds expectations.

- *Specialized training and education.* The completion of specialized training or education programs can be an important requirement. Such training can represent new areas of competence for the trainer's organization.

- *Willingness to share.* Trainers should have a temperament that enables them to share their experiences and competence with others. They should be interested in the development of other employees.

- *Respect of peers.* Many trainers are already perceived by other employees as having special status as a result of their higher level of competence, leadership abilities, general problem-solving skills, or knowledge of the organization.

- *Interpersonal skills.* Interpersonal skills involve the individual's ability to express complex ideas clearly and comprehensively during everyday interactions.

- *Literacy skills.* Every trainer must be able to comprehend resource materials or perform calculations related to the unit of work.

- *Concern for the organization.* Trainers should show an interest in helping the organization improve its performance. They can demonstrate such an interest by participating in continuous improvement efforts, following safe work practices, and doing things that help the organization achieve its goals.

- *Work expectations.* Some experienced employees have work expectations or assignments that require them to become a S-OJT trainer.

The importance of the criteria just reviewed is likely to differ with the unit of work being considered for training. While adequate competence in the work can be the most important criterion to consider in some instances, it is not necessarily the most important criteria for all situations. For example, tasks involving highly technical information logically require the selection process to emphasize the employees who possess task knowledge, possibly at the expense of other criteria. But tasks that contain more general information, as they do when the training content describes a work process, may require trainers to have less task knowledge than other criteria, such as concern for the organization. Ultimately, management in cooperation with supervisors and job incumbents should determine the best mix of criteria for a given unit of work.

Table 6.1 presents a trainer qualification checklist that organizations may use to rate individuals who seek to become S-OJT trainers. The checklist asks that raters judge the level of competence required for the unit of work and the level of competence observed in the individual being rated. The checklist helps when more than one judge is being used to rate the prospective trainers.

TABLE 6.1. Trainer Qualification Checklist

Name: _____ ID: _____

Department: _____ Title: _____

Unit of Work: _____

Criteria	Level of Competence Required	Level of Competence Observed	Comment
A. Adequate competence in the work			
B. Specialized training and education			
C. Willingness to share			
D. Respect of peers			
E. Interpersonal skills			
F. Literacy/language skills			
G. Concern for the organization			
H. Work expectations			
I. Completion of train-the-trainer course			

Levels: (1) expert; (2) advanced specialist; (3) specialist.

_____ has successfully met the criteria to conduct S-OJT on this unit of work.

Signed: _____
  Department Head   Date

Signed: _____
  HRD Manager   Date

Selecting the Trainers

Typically, the employees who have held a job the longest or who have the highest status in the work areas are the ones asked to be trainers. However, reliance on the selection criteria reviewed in the preceding section has the effect of involving more employees in the training and of bringing a wider variety of individuals into the training process. In this sense, the selection criteria can involve employees who in the past have not had an opportunity to be trainers.

Once you have settled on the selection criteria, you can select prospective S-OJT trainers from one or the other of two basic groups of employees: *staff trainers* who are already adept at the training process, such as members of their HRD staff, or subject-matter experts who are specifically hired to conduct the training; and *experienced employees*, including supervisors and front-line employees, who should attain an appropriate level of competence in the training process.

It is impossible to say that one group is better in all instances, because much depends on factors within the organization and nature of the work. Those who favor using only staff trainers make the point that this practice limits work disruptions, because line employees do not have to drop what they are doing to conduct the training. They add that since work locations can vary, it is easier to send staff trainers to the trainees' location than it is to bring trainees to trainers. In such instances, the training can involve prolonged contact between the trainer and trainee, perhaps up to several months of continuous training and practice sessions. Many organizations use itinerant S-OJT trainers. Finally, reliance on staff trainers minimizes the risk of violating contractual agreements that prevent employees from undertaking training responsibilities.

While these are compelling reasons, it is not always appropriate to use staff trainers in all instances. Many more organizations are moving toward having experienced employees become trainers. One major advantage of this approach is that these individuals possess in-depth knowledge of the work. Needless to say, staff trainers cannot be expected to be proficient in every unit of work in an organization or work area for which training is required. Moreover, even when staff trainers do have sufficient competence in the work, the depth of their knowledge is likely to decline, because only those who perform the work continuously can know all its ins and outs.

Another advantage of using experienced employees as trainers is that the practice spreads the training responsibility out among more employees. The ideal of a learning organization remains only an ideal unless as many individuals as possible become actively involved in sharing what they know and can do with others. One critical factor in the drive to achieve training objectives is the trainee's receptiveness to learning the knowledge and skills. Often, trainees are more willing to accept information from people who actually perform the work and who can provide additional guidance as needed.

Sometimes staff should be used instead of experienced employees. Moreover, not every experienced employee is capable of becoming a trainer. That is, many experienced employees are simply not interested in becoming involved in any way, or their superiors may deem their talents better used elsewhere in the organization. Still others may want to become a trainer but do not meet certain selection criteria (Leach, 1991).

Once the criteria have been identified, the selection of trainers can proceed in any one of a variety of ways:

- *General announcement.* An announcement can be made throughout the organization encouraging interested employees to sign up for consideration. Managers and human resources staff can apply the selection criteria chosen by the organization to the individuals who respond to this call. This approach can attract a fairly wide cadre of qualified trainers who represent both line and staff areas.

- *Nomination.* Supervisors and managers can nominate certain individuals who have the appropriate competence in the work that have been identified for S-OJT. Some of these individuals may already be known if they served as subject-matter experts during the work analysis.

- *Recruiting.* Line managers, first-line supervisors, or advanced-level front-line employees may be actively recruited as S-OJT trainers. Furthermore, the selection criteria for being a S-OJT trainer may be used when considering whether to promote or develop certain employees.

Whichever of these approaches is selected, the usual next step is to interview candidates or have them participate in simulations. For example, prospective S-OJT trainers can be asked to demonstrate a simple procedure, such as assembling a flashlight, or give a presentation to explain an organization-related topic. Their performance can be rated according to some criteria, such as their comfort in speaking in front of others. The final selection decisions can be based on the resulting information.

The last issue related to the selection of trainers concerns the matching of trainers and trainees. Such matching is commonly based on some variable of importance, such as the individuals' respective backgrounds, styles, or attitudes. While this issue can affect the success of training, care taken in regard to other parts of the system can make up for many of these differences. Research from a number of different perspectives has assessed the effects of matches or mismatches between individuals in social situations. Matching has not conclusively been shown to improve outcomes. While it seems evident that individuals can sense when they share something with those around them, they often cannot articulate the precise nature of their commonalities.

In practice, the selection of individuals to serve as S-OJT trainers often faces more constraints than the preceding discussion suggests. No more than one or two individuals may have sufficient competence in a given unit of work. Or there may be constraints on who is actually available. No matter what the constraints, it is important to both the organization and the employees selected that specific criteria be used to select the S-OJT trainers.

Training the Trainers

Once the trainers have been selected, they need to undergo a focused training and development program that will give them the knowledge and skills to deliver S-OJT. Most organizations eventually design their own programs, primarily because the commercially available programs inherently lack the necessary depth, relevance, and fit with other parts of the organization's S-OJT effort. In addition, becoming an S-OJT trainer requires much different skills than becoming a classroom instructor. While similar in many respects, the emphasis and context of S-OJT makes it different from most other training situations in which a trainer is involved.

Programs used to train S-OJT trainers should include the following objectives:

- State the features of S-OJT.
- Predict the organizational consequences of using structured and unstructured OJT.
- Demonstrate how to analyze work in which they have competence (optional).
- Show how to prepare various components of S-OJT modules (optional).
- Demonstrate how to get ready for delivering S-OJT.

- Demonstrate the ability to deliver S-OJT by making use of the appropriate instructional events.
- Apply criteria to evaluate the effectiveness of their own training.

If no relevant modules are available for use in the trainer-training program, the organization may ask trainees to help develop the modules as part of the program itself. While this expectation may seem to place an undue burden on them, it does have at least two advantages. First, having a meaningful context may well help experienced employees become more effective trainers. Second, experienced employees often have greater feelings of ownership since they participate in the development of the training.

The amount of time required to achieve these objectives is usually twelve hours of group-based training, making use of printed workbooks, videotaped examples of case studies, and various small-group activities. At the conclusion of the in-class experience, each trainee delivers at least one of the S-OJT modules that he or she will be expected to deliver later on the job.

People often ask whether S-OJT is appropriate for training S-OJT trainers. The answer is that it can be appropriate when only one or two individuals require such training but that it is usually better to train trainers in a classroom setting. Such a setting makes it possible for trainees to receive feedback from peers and discuss the organizational implications of using S-OJT.

Appendix B presents a rating form used to judge trainer performance. The form has multiple uses. During the training, it can be used to establish trainer expectations. It can also be used to guide practice and feedback and to follow up with trainers after the training has been completed. In some organizations, the development experience is not considered to be complete until the trainee is observed delivering a S-OJT module in the actual work setting. Only after successfully completing all the activities is the employee qualified to deliver S-OJT. Some organizations formalize the successful completion of these objectives by awarding a certificate of accomplishment.

Managing Trainer Performance

Once a group of experienced employees is qualified as trainers, the organization needs to consider how to maintain and improve their performance over time. Any discussion of these issues should first acknowledge that different individuals have different motives for becoming a trainer. Some persons seek to become trainers for strictly personal reasons, such as the opportunity to gain the respect of others. Others may be motivated by organizational incentives, such as opportunities for development, status, recognition, pay, or promotion. The organization's managers and employee representatives should decide what rewards are appropriate.

Experience suggests the following points about maintaining and improving trainer performance. First, while individuals may have different motives for becoming a trainer, the organization should take specific actions to maintain the strength of those motives over time. Becoming a trainer involves the expense of additional time and effort, which may not be apparent to some employees at first. The initial interest can be dampened by the unexpected amount of work involved in becoming a trainer.

Second, although the use of financial incentives can be appropriate in certain circumstances, as when becoming a trainer also involves an upgrade in role or promotion, it is in general terms to be discouraged. For one thing, some positions may actually require the individual to act as a trainer. Additional incentives are not appropriate in such cases. Second, financial rewards can needlessly complicate the situation, since giving differential pay to employees can involve contractual or personnel issues. Moreover, it is likely that the same trainer performance can be achieved through offerings that are nonfinancial in nature.

Third, certain low-key recognition techniques and regularly scheduled opportunities for professional development usually satisfy the needs of most employees. Organizations use a number of nonfinancial rewards with success:

- Specially printed coffee cups, pins, or caps denoting that the person is a qualified trainer

- Certificates that may be hung in an office or work area

- Follow-up meetings that give trainers an opportunity to discuss the various individual issues and concerns they may have as a result of conducting the training

- Meetings at which trainers and managers can discuss ways of improving the use of S-OJT

- Permission to attend professional meetings and conferences off-site that focus on S-OJT and other related topics

- Periodic feedback sessions based on observations of trainers during the delivery of S-OJT

All the nonfinancial incentives just listed are designed to maintain and improve trainer performance. At the very least, becoming an S-OJT trainer should not place an undue burden on the employee. That would defeat the purpose of the entire effort. To prevent the trainer role from becoming a burden, management should be prepared to provide the additional resources necessary to cover trainers when they participate in training activities outside of their work area.

The summary sheet in Figure 6.1 is designed to guide the trainer development process. Because the effectiveness of S-OJT depends so strongly on the quality of trainers, the trainer development process should involve as many groups as possible, including management, staff, and appropriate employee representatives.

A. Identifying selection criteria (check those that apply for the unit of work)
   1. Adequate competence in the work _____
   2. Specialized training and education _____
   3. Willingness to share _____
   4. Respect of peers _____
   5. Interpersonal skills _____
   6. Literacy skills _____
   7. Concern for the organization _____
   8. Work expectations _____

B. Selecting the trainers (identify groups who will train)
   1. Staff trainers _____
   2. Line managers _____
   3. Front-line employees _____

C. Training the trainers (select objectives of the training)
   1. Understand S-OJT _____
   2. Understand unstructured OJT _____
   3. Conduct work analysis _____
   4. Prepare S-OJT modules _____
   5. Deliver S-OJT _____
   6. Evaluate trainer effectiveness _____

D. Managing trainer performance (incentives for trainers)
   1. Coffee cups, pins, caps, and so on _____
   2. Meetings among trainers _____
   3. Professional meetings off-site _____
   4. Direct observations of trainers _____

FIGURE 6.1. S-OJT Trainer Development Summary Sheet

CERTIFICATION OF S-OJT TRAINERS

The question often arises whether a certification should be given to the S-OJT trainers. This consideration rests with the organization and the nature of the requirements placed on it. In general, certification suggests that the trainer has achieved some level of accomplishment, which increases the reliability of the trainer's performance in delivering the S-OJT. Some caution should be exercised in undertaking the certification of trainers, however.

If certification means that the trainer has completed a train-the-trainer course alone, then this meaning is too limited. To be meaningful, trainer certification means that the individual has completed the train-the-trainer course and has been observed delivering the training under actual circumstances, using a rating form such as that presented in Appendix B. Thus, seeking trainer certification extends the development process long past the conclusion of the train-the-trainer course.

Instead of trainer certification, a preferred term is *trainer qualification*. In that way, organizations can decide the extent to which trainers will be asked to perform before they are allowed to train others. Also, the term *trainer qualification* may lessen liability risks often associated with training.

CONCLUSION

In S-OJT, experienced employees present important work-related knowledge and skills to other persons. That is why it is important to develop experienced employees as trainers. This chapter has presented a four-step process that addresses the development of S-OJT trainers. To a large extent, the effectiveness of S-OJT depends on involving the best employees as trainers. *Best* depends on the criteria selected for trainers in a given unit of work. Using front-line employees close to the work improves the transfer of the information within the organization, and it gives the organization an opportunity to provide job enrichment for deserving employees.

Chapter 7
Preparing the Structured On-the-Job Training Modules

S-OJT is superior to most other forms of training that occur in the work setting chiefly because it is structured. The structure helps it achieve the desired training objectives more efficiently and effectively each time it is used. The training modules used in S-OJT contribute much to its success. The following topics are discussed in this chapter:

- The components and formats of S-OJT modules
- Three types of training
- The preparation of S-OJT modules

STRUCTURED ON-THE-JOB TRAINING MODULES

The sets of instructional materials that accompany S-OJT programs are called *modules*. An S-OJT module is an organized package that contains all the information necessary to deliver training. Like a lesson plan, an S-OJT module documents the training content and addresses the delivery of the training. However, since S-OJT can be delivered by a variety of individuals, the typical S-OJT module is both

111

more comprehensive and more self-contained than a traditional lesson plan.

In practice, S-OJT modules are the documents that trainers and trainees have in hand during the training process. As explained in Chapters 8 and 9, trainers use the modules as they get ready to deliver the training, as reference when they deliver the training, and as they rate the performance of trainees after training. Trainees receive a slightly modified version of the modules so that they can preview the training content and objectives before training, follow the trainer during training, and review what they are expected to perform after training. When S-OJT modules are used in these ways, they play an important role in ensuring the success of training.

Module Components

Most S-OJT modules include the following basic components:

Title
The title presents the content of the module in explicit terms. To promote consistency and clarity, the module title should follow directly from the unit of work or the information on which the training content is based.

Rationale Statement
The rationale statement tells the trainee why the training is important by stating what the trainee can do with the information that he or she acquires in the training. The rationale statement should also focus on the importance of the information to the development of the individual employee or the organization's effort to attain long-term goals.

Training Objectives
The training objectives specify what the trainee should know or be able to do as a result of the training. As ex-

plained in Chapter 5, training objectives should be referenced to work expectations. In preparing the module, you may find it useful to state the training objective in terms familiar to the targeted trainees, such as by using a "statement of purpose" instead of a "training objective." Both the trainer and the trainee should understand the meaning of the training objectives

Training Prerequisites

Training prerequisites are the knowledge, skills, and attitudes that trainees must possess on entering the training session. Trainees have obtained this information from previous training programs, or from work experiences. Trainers use these prerequisites to determine the readiness of trainees for training. It also helps trainees determine their own readiness for training.

Training Resources

Since training occurs in the work setting, trainers should gather together any data, equipment, tools, and instructional materials that training calls for. The scheduling of S-OJT often depends on the availability of resources. Resources used in ongoing work of the organization will have to be taken offline so that training can be conducted. Specifying the resources needed for training in the module itself helps limit interruptions in training while a trainer looks for, say, a document or a tool.

Training Content

The training module should document the training content completely. The training content can be presented in a variety of ways, depending on the nature of the work. Training guides are extremely useful for procedural, troubleshooting, inspection, and decision-making tasks—indeed, for any unit of work that requires a trainee to learn how to apply a technical skill or conceptual information (Rossett & Gautier-Downes, 1991). Work that involves concepts or principles may require instead that training content be represented in a structured text format (Jonassen, 1982).

In most cases, it is preferable for a module to combine training guides and structured text materials. Flexibility in presenting the training content is encouraged.

Training Events

How should training be delivered? This is the question that trainers most often ask—understandably, for them it is the most visible part of S-OJT. Training events describe how to deliver S-OJT to trainees in the most effective way. As described in Chapter 8, delivery of S-OJT typically involves five training events:

1. Prepare the trainee.
2. Present the training.
3. Require a response.
4. Provide feedback.
5. Evaluate performance.

Performance Tests and Feedback Forms

At the conclusion of training, the trainer should certify that a trainee has successfully achieved the training objectives. Thus, most modules include performance tests, such as performance-rating scales (product scales or process scales) or cognitive tests. A module can also contain forms that document the completion of training and provide summative feedback certifying that the training objectives have been achieved.

Organizations use this information in different ways. Some organizations purposely integrate this information as part of the employee's developmental plan and require that the information be maintained in a formal way. Other organizations use the forms only for employee feedback. However, an increasing number of organizations use the feedback forms for personnel planning and employee development. In

TABLE 7.1. Example Training Schedule			
TRAINING SCHEDULE			
Prepared for:		*Date:*	
Prepared by:		*Revised:*	
Module	*Date Started*	*Date Finished*	*Trainer*
a. Conducting a performance appraisal session	_____	_____	_____
b. Resolving conflicts between employees	_____	_____	_____
c. Scheduling customer orders	_____	_____	_____
d. Conducting team meetings	_____	_____	_____

these organizations, when a trainee completes training, copies of the completed forms are sent to the trainee's supervisor or to human resource staff, so that the employee's development record can be updated. How the rating forms are used often depends on the nature of the work, the requirements of the organization's customers, or the potential consequences of error when the work is performed.

Table 7.1 shows a training schedule that one organization uses to document the completion of S-OJT modules. Completed training schedules become part of the trainee's development plan.

An increasing number of organizations require employees to become certified in the performance of certain work that is critical to the achievement of organizational outcomes. Many of these organizations certify employees to comply with meeting ISO 9000 quality standards. One effective way of meeting customer requirements is to use performance-rating scales with S-OJT.

Additional Information

A training module can also include additional information that serves to supplement or enrich the training content. This additional information can include such things as internal technical documents, blueprints, customer satisfaction data, safety manuals, technical documents, or reprints from professional magazines and journals.

Module Formats

Once the module's components have been prepared, the next step is to determine the format in which they should be assembled. Five different formats are possible: short form, spiral-bound booklet, three-ring binder, printed booklet with permanent binding, and embedded text.

Short Form

The simplest and most expedient format for a S-OJT module is the short form, which consists of just one or very few pages. Modules in this format can be prepared in relatively little time and the cost is low. This format seems especially suited when the unit of work is relatively short in length or has few complications, when resources are limited, or when the unit of work or the information presented is expected to change soon. Laminated card stock is used for the pages.

For one organization alone, twenty short-form modules were prepared. These modules were stored in metal book racks in the work setting. The location made the modules easily accessible. Each module was available in two versions. Trainers used one version as reference during training and put it back on the rack when the training was completed. Trainees used a giveaway version before training. They were instructed to review the information before training and to refer to it during training. Many employees kept the module after training for reference.

Some caution should be taken not to overuse this format. The short form is effective for many situations, but not for all. It is always a challenge to maintain the details and complexity of training content while presenting them in a way that makes the information accessible and useful. This format can tempt one to oversimplify the training content, and oversimplification runs the risk of omitting critical information. A thorough analysis of the unit of work is still a prerequisite when the short form is used.

Spiral-Bound Booklet

One step up from the short form is the spiral-bound booklet. The spiral binding is located lengthwise on a full sheet of standard-size paper or on the short side of standard paper cut in half. Both cover and pages are most often made of stiff card stock. This format seems especially suited when the training content involves complex actions, such as lengthy procedures or complex troubleshooting.

The spiral-bound booklet is more permanent than the short form. Its usefulness may be limited for some training content, such as detailed text information. The horizontal aspect ratio enables the spiral-bound booklet to be propped up at the workstation, and the employee has both hands free to perform the work. The spiral-bound booklet seems best suited to situations in which the trainee and the trainer can use the module from a distance.

Three-Ring Binder

The three-ring binder format makes it possible to present structured text information along with a variety of accompanying resources. For example, in addition to text information, a three-ring binder can easily hold folded blueprints, schematics, or other large reference materials. It can also accommodate an appendix section for enrichment materials that could be shared with trainees after training. Finally, a binder can include zippered pockets holding small tools and materials, such as slide rules and micrometers, and other materials that are part of the training content.

These additional resources are usually considered to be dedicated parts of the module. They should not be removed for other purposes. Having the training resources readily available in the module allows flexibility and creativity when the trainer presents the training, when the trainee practices and responds to the training, and when the trainer evaluates the trainee's performance. A self-contained module facilitates all these activities. The three-ring binder format has two possible disadvantages if many copies of the module are required: the costs of the binders and the resources that go in the binders.

Printed Booklet with Permanent Binding

If the training content is unlikely to change and if many trainees will require training, then a printed booklet with permanent binding can be the most appropriate format. This format can present several different varieties of training content. However, the permanent binding limits its flexibility. Nonetheless, modules in this format can be produced at relatively low cost when large numbers of copies are required.

Embedded Text

Finally, if the S-OJT involves the use of computers, it is possible to present the training content as embedded text. Embedded format can be used in conjunction with internal menu prompts or off-the-shelf computer shells that can be purchased to accompany many commercially produced software programs. In most cases, modules in this format are used in conjunction with materials in some other format, such as a spiral-bound booklet or short form.

The embedded format seems most suitable when the S-OJT involves learning a task that is performed on or with the assistance of a computer. Many bank tellers, for example, acquire the knowledge and skills required to do various operations directly from their computer screens. The work and S-OJT are combined in one training medium.

TYPES OF TRAINING

Traditionally, OJT has been perceived as most appropriate for training semiskilled employees to perform technical tasks in production settings (Stokes, 1966). Even today, training a newly hired machine operator through OJT projects a powerful image to managers. This image is now largely inaccurate. S-OJT can be used for many other types of training. Most notably, S-OJT can be used successfully for delivering managerial, technical, and awareness training. Table 7.2 defines the three types of training and the associated performance outcomes.

Managerial Training

When S-OJT is used to present managerial training, it gives trainees the ability to plan, direct, or facilitate others' efforts (Mafi, 2001). These skills enable employees to do such work as resolve conflicts, schedule work activities, facilitate team meetings, and provide feedback. While managerial training does not represent the actual work done in the organization, it is nevertheless important to the organization. Managerial training helps organizations make the work happen.

The changing nature of work means that managerial training is not necessarily restricted to managers and supervisors. It is appropriate for front-line employees. Consider that managers and supervisors now receive large amounts of technical training in addition to managerial training. At the same time, front-line hourly employees now receive increasing amounts of managerial training in addition to

TABLE 7.2. Types of Training

Training Type	Description	Performance Outcomes
MANAGERIAL	Gives the trainee the ability to plan, direct, or facilitate the efforts of others	Written or oral skills to ensure that goals are met, projects are completed, and work gets done
TECHNICAL	Gives the trainee the ability to manipulate objects, equipment, tools, data, or some other resources in some way	Finished products or services, usually tangible in nature
AWARENESS	Informs the trainee about ideas, processes, or policies presently used in the organization or motivates the trainee to accept planned change in some aspect of the organization	Ability to state ideas in his or her own words or show commitment by the consistency between words and actions

technical training. Indeed, all levels of employees are now likely to receive some type of managerial training.

Here are some titles of S-OJT modules that involve managerial training:

- Providing Subordinate Feedback
- Facilitating Team Meetings
- Identifying Customer Requirements
- Planning Employee Work Schedules
- Conducting a Performance Appraisal

These titles suggest that managerial training requires that trainees should first understand underlying concepts and principles, often represented as a model or a process, and then apply that information through the use of various communication techniques. Thus, the outcomes of managerial training are often expressed by the oral or written behaviors of trainees.

Technical Training

When S-OJT is used to present technical training, it gives trainees the ability to manipulate objects, equipment, tools, data, or other resources in some way to achieve the training objectives. In general, technical training enables employees to perform a wide range of tasks, from machine operation and document preparation, to sales and customer service techniques. Technical training also includes many safety and quality techniques. Technical training is the most frequent type of training in organizations.

Here are some titles that involve technical training:

- Operating the Bolt-Maker Machine
- Inspecting Purchase Order Contracts
- Completing Purchase Order Forms
- Making Contact with Sales Prospects
- Troubleshooting a Financial Audit
- Designing an Electrical Circuit

As these module titles show, the outcomes that result from technical training are more often than not tangible products or services. To produce these products or services, employees combine psychomotor skills or verbal chains (the linking together of physical or verbal information) with intellectual. Many people mistakenly believe that technical training is only about psychomotor skills or verbal chains. In fact, concepts and principles play an important part in technical training. In many cases, concepts and principles are best learned in an off-the-job training program or should be considered prerequisites to the training.

Awareness Training

Finally, when S-OJT is used to present awareness training, it can have one or both of two outcomes. The trainee is informed about ideas, processes, or policies that are presently used in the organization, or the trainee is motivated to accept some type of planned change in the organization. Because awareness training usually focuses on information rather than on specific units of work, the outcomes of awareness training are more often cognitive in nature than the outcomes of managerial and technical training. Nevertheless, from the organization's perspective, it is critical for the trainee to have this information.

Here are some titles of S-OJT modules that involve the informational aspect of awareness training:

- Selecting a Profit-Sharing Plan
- Understanding Customer Requirements
- Understanding the Customer Service Workflow
- Knowing Your Role in the Continuous Improvement Process

Here are some titles of S-OJT modules that involve the motivational aspect of awareness training:

- Orienting Union Members
- Committing to the New Pull Production System
- Working as a Team Member
- Using SPC as a Management Tool
- Managing in the New Organization

At times, managerial and awareness training may seem indistinguishable. They can be differentiated by asking, Does the training content represent information that is directly related to a work expectation? If the answer is yes, the training is likely to be managerial. If the answer is no, the training is likely to be awareness. The importance of this distinction may not be apparent, but type of training does affect the outcomes of training. Managerial training usually requires a trainee to be able to do something as a result of training, while awareness training requires a trainee to know about something at the end of the training.

Implications for S-OJT

The three types of training have important implications for the preparation and delivery of S-OJT modules. A characteristic set of training activities is associated with each type of training. Moreover, these training activities can be organized around a basic instructional pattern, which is often referred to as *whole-part-whole*. Thus, type of training affects the instructional pattern. Table 7.3 was adapted from Swanson and Law (1993) and shows how the whole-part-whole pattern can be applied to managerial, technical, and awareness training programs.

In practical terms, the whole-part-whole design pattern resembles the dictum "Tell them what you're going to teach. Teach them. Then tell them what you've taught them." In fact, the whole-part-whole design pattern borrows from at least two different learning perspectives.

First, the whole component provides a sense of the bigger picture or broad context in which the training content is embedded. It also explains the relationship between the broad context and the work or the set of information to be learned. Hartley and Davies (1976) refer to the techniques used to accomplish the first whole component as *preinstructional strategies*. One of the best known of these strategies is the advance organizers introduced by Ausubel (1968). Advance organizers make it possible to learn verbal information through the introduction of related information before the training.

TABLE 7.3. Whole-Part-Whole Training Pattern			
Type of Training	*First Whole*	*Part*	*Second Whole*
MANAGERIAL	▪ Purpose ▪ Examples ▪ Overview of model or process	▪ Components of model or process ▪ Techniques to apply model or process ▪ Decision making	▪ Practice ▪ Role plays ▪ State implications
TECHNICAL	▪ Purpose ▪ Overview of workflow ▪ Overview of operation	▪ Start-up ▪ Operation ▪ Shutdown ▪ Inspection ▪ Maintenance ▪ Adjustments or revisions	▪ Troubleshooting ▪ Decision making ▪ Practice ▪ Integration of parts
AWARENESS	▪ Purpose ▪ Problem condition ▪ Consequences of current situation ▪ Opportunities of desired situation	▪ Personal actions needed to achieve the desired situation	▪ Commitment statement to change

Source: Based on Swanson and Law (1993).

The part component presents the information specific to the learning task. The parts are the details of the training, the individual pieces of information that the trainee must master in order to acquire the appropriate level of competence. Learning of the parts can sometimes be facilitated by careful sequencing and by breaking the content down into small logical units. Each unit should be learned individually in order to achieve the entire behaviors called for in the training objective. This approach draws on the behavioral learning perspective.

The individual units of training content within the part component can often be sequenced by one of the principles: simple content to complex content, known content to unknown content, or concrete content to abstract content

The second whole component connects the individual parts of the training content and shows their relationships. It also promotes insights into the work that are available only as a result of learning the parts. In effect, the second whole gives meaning to the parts through rehearsal. When the trainer requires the trainee to put it all together, he or she asks the trainee to produce behaviors. Producing the behaviors as part of training helps the trainee to learn and retain the information.

The fact that S-OJT relies on experienced employees as trainers gives the whole-part-whole special importance. When experienced employees are left to their own devices, most omit the first whole component. Moreover, when delivering the training, they can omit parts that they mistakenly assume to be obvious or self-evident. Finally, they seldom include the second whole component, since they do not explicitly realize the importance that this information has for others.

As stated, the whole-part-whole design pattern helps organize training activities for the different types of training. In practice, a single S-OJT lesson can present more than one type of training, which means that some creative programming will be needed. For example, learning why it is important to follow a specific procedure to lock out a piece of equipment is awareness training. But learning the steps of the lockout procedure is technical training. One would seldom train a person on one topic without the other. Logically, learning about safety and learning to do things in a safe way go hand in hand.

Thus, in order for a trainee to have a meaningful learning experience, the training activities that relate to each type of training need to be combined creatively.

PREPARATION OF THE S-OJT MODULES

The preparation of a S-OJT module is a matter of combining the work information and the appropriate whole-part-whole design pattern into a finished product. Of critical importance is the integration of training content and type of training. This issue can be addressed in either of the two ways described here.

Separate Training Events from Training Content

In some modules, especially modules for technical training, the training events are best separated from the training content. Since technical training usually involves the learning of procedures, decision making, or troubleshooting information, the training content is presented in printed form as a job performance guide. Figure 7.1 shows how the training events are printed on a separate laminated card to be used alongside the job performance guide.

In practice, the trainer can decide either to position the card so that it can be referred to throughout the training—for example, by placing it on a clipboard—or to keep the card within reach and use it as needed. For this reason, cards are prepared in ways to ensure their flexibility. Sometimes, the card is prepared to fit the shape of a shirt pocket, tool kit, or some other convenient storage location in the work setting.

Embed Training Events in Training Content

In many modules, especially for managerial and awareness training, it is not appropriate to separate training events from training content. In these modules, the training content is likely to consist of conceptual information as well

Training Steps

1. **Prepare trainee**
   a. Determine trainee readiness
   b. Explain training process
   c. Explain bigger picture
   d. Respond to questions

2. **Present training**
   a. Position the trainee
   b. Review task
   c. Show and tell each part
   d. Summarize task

3. **Require response**
   a. Ask for review
   b. Ask for show and tell
   c. Ask for summary

4. **Provide feedback**
   a. Require logical chain
   b. Provide coaching
   c. Point out helpful cues

5. **Evaluate performance**
   a. Ask for self-report
   b. Rate performance
   c. Record completion

FIGURE 7.1. Training Events Reference Card

as of processes and decision making. When these types of information are combined, they often show a close relationship between particular aspects of the training content and the associated training event. As a result, two versions of the S-OJT module are often needed: a trainee's version that presents the training content only and a trainer's version that includes both training content and detailed information based on the five training events used to deliver the content.

As Appendix D shows, embedding the training events in the training content can be integrated with the format used in structured text approaches. The example is taken from a portion of an S-OJT module entitled "Responding to Guest Complaints" for guest relations representatives in a hotel chain. The embedded information informs the trainer on how to deliver the information in the module. In this way, the trainer can both present the content—much of it would be a summary of the text information—and refer to specific delivery information, such as key words to emphasize or suggest examples. The training was conducted by experienced supervisors or managers and used in conjunction with an off-the-job training program that introduces other aspects of the delegation process.

To summarize, S-OJT modules serve as the primary reference for trainer and trainee. Thus, judgments about the adequacy of a module should not be based on its appearance. Expensive binding and color graphics are often unnecessary, and they add to training cost. In fact, training materials all too often end up sitting on a shelf in someone's office and get little actual use. The emphasis needs to be placed not on the form but on the usefulness of the training materials. Once the module is prepared in final form, the S-OJT is ready for delivery by the experienced employee.

CONCLUSION

S-OJT modules are the instructional materials that combine training content with instructions on how to deliver the training. The instructions on how to deliver the training are based on the five training events. The major components of S-OJT modules are relatively consistent. S-OJT can be used for three types of training. A whole-part-whole pattern underlies the design of the materials used in all three types of training.

Chapter 8

Getting Ready to Deliver Structured On-the-Job Training

When the training module has been prepared, the S-OJT is ready to be delivered on demand. The trainer's actions to get ready are part of delivering S-OJT. This chapter presents the following information:

- The training events used for delivering S-OJT
- The steps to take when preparing to deliver S-OJT

TRAINING EVENTS

Chapter 7 identified the five training events for S-OJT:

1. Prepare the trainee.
2. Present the content.
3. Require a response.
4. Provide feedback.
5. Evaluate performance.

This chapter describes them in depth. Training events ensure that the trainer uses the sequence and techniques appropriate to the learning that trainees should experience. In other words, training events ensure that trainers use the most effective external activities to bring about the most predictable internal events (Gagne et al., 1988).

Today, when companies seek a standard way of delivering OJT, most adopt some variation of the four-step method as originally proposed by Allen during World War I and further refined as part of the Training within Industry (TWI) effort during World War II. The four steps are logical, easy to remember, and effective (Dooley, 1945). Yet, by their very nature of the four steps, they tend to reinforce the notion that OJT is restricted to the learning of hands-on, technical information. Because the view of human competence is expanding in organizations, the training events should be amended in some essential ways.

Social Learning Theory

At first glance, the five training events may seem to be based more on commonsense logic than on anything else. In fact, they are based on widely accepted principles of social learning theory. Social learning theory assumes that, when individuals are exposed to a model, the stimuli that they receive from the model is coded and retained by them in order to guide the performance of the modeled response (Bandura, 1978). In other words, what trainees remember will become coded instructions to themselves when they attempt later on to reproduce the modeled behavior. The degree of learning is affected by a trainee's attentional, retentional, reproduction, and reinforcement processes.

The paragraphs that follow relate social learning theory to the training events of S-OJT:

1. *Prepare the trainee.* The first event focuses the trainee's attention to the topic at hand, creates an atmosphere conducive to learning, gives meaning to the topic, and establishes standards of performance. Of

special importance to S-OJT, this event has been shown to reduce learning anxiety and increase the ability of trainees to learn the training content later on (Gomersall & Myers, 1966).

2. *Present the training.* The second event serves to guide the attention of the trainee toward specific parts of the training content. For these cues to be understood, the trainer needs to make them as visible and as distinct as possible. For this reason, the trainer should separate the training content into small components. Trainees can attend more effectively to behaviors that are made more available to them.

3. *Require a response.* The third event calls for trainees to respond in a meaningful way to the model that was presented. Requiring an active response helps trainees retain content. Rehearsing the modeled behavior enhances retention, because it helps trainees develop personal codes of the modeled behavior. Also, it helps expose information that was overlooked during the presentation of the content. In other words, making an active response helps the trainees internalize the training content and give it personal meaning.

4. *Provide feedback.* The fourth training event requires the trainer to provide trainees with pertinent information about the accuracy and adequacy of their responses. This information serves to identify the areas in which additional practice and improvement are required. Extensive behavioral research over the past fifty years has formulated some principles on the giving of feedback. In general, feedback that is to the point and either immediate or slightly delayed is preferable in most training situations. Ultimately, a trainee's ability to reproduce the modeled behavior is facilitated by feedback from the trainer.

5. *Evaluate performance*. The fifth training event is a summative judgment of the adequacy of the trainee's performance. The training event gives the trainee a sense of satisfaction by demonstrating that he or she has learned the modeled behavior according to an established standard. This event also ensures that a trainee will consider how the learned behavior transfers to the work. Finally, it ensures that the trainee's performance has undergone a summative judgment by the trainer, which can be documented in the trainee's development plan or personnel record. The quality improvement movement has placed increasing emphasis on the fifth training event.

Training Events and Types of Training

The five training events should be viewed as generic activities. That is, the specific activities to which the events correspond depend on the particular type of training: managerial, technical, and awareness.

Figure 8.1 presents the five training events and the respective actions for each type of training. The training events apply the whole-part-whole instructional pattern described in Chapter 7. In practice, two events present the greatest differences: when the content is presented to the trainee and when the trainee is required to respond. It is not the intent to overcomplicate the seemingly straightforward activity of delivering training content. Rather, the purpose is to show that different types of training require different training design and that these designs need to be based on the characteristics of the training content. Chapter 9 describes how to use the training events to deliver each type of training.

PREPARING DELIVERY

Before S-OJT can be delivered, certain activities have to occur: The training has to be scheduled, training resources

Managerial Training

1. Prepare the trainee
   a. Explain the purpose and rationale of the training.
   b. Determine whether the trainee has the prerequisites.
   c. Explain general safety and quality requirements.
   d. Explain how the training will be done.
   e. Ask if trainee has any questions about the training.

2. Present the training
   a. Position the trainee
   b. Present an overview of the model, process, or project.
   c. Present examples of the model, process, or project.
   d. Explain parts of the model, process, or project.
   e. Explain techniques to apply the model, process, or project.
   f. Demonstrate techniques to apply the model, process, or project.
   g. Summarize the entire model, process, or project.

3. Require a response
   a. Ask the trainee to present an overview of the model, process, or project.
   b. Ask the trainee for examples of the model, process, or project.
   c. Ask the trainee to explain parts of the model, process, or project.
   d. Ask the trainee to explain techniques to apply the model, process, or project.
   e. Ask the trainee to demonstrate techniques to apply model, process, or project.
   f. Ask the trainee to summarize the entire model, process, or project.

4. Provide feedback
   a. Inform the trainee about the adequacy of responses.
   b. Provide coaching and guidance at points of error.
   c. Point out embedded cues in the work setting.

5. Evaluate performance
   a. Evaluate the trainee's self-report.
   b. Evaluate performance test results.
   c. Document the trainee's performance.   *continued*

FIGURE 8.1. Training Events and Types of Training

Technical Training

1. Prepare the trainee
   a. Explain the purpose and rationale of the training.
   b. Determine whether the trainee has the prerequisites.
   c. Explain general safety and quality requirements.
   d. Explain how the training will be done.
   e. Ask if trainee has any questions about the training.

2. Present the training
   a. Position the trainee.
   b. Present an overview of the operation, equipment, or workflow.
   c. Present an overview of the unit of work.
   d. Tell and show each behavior.
   e. Explain specific safety and quality points.
   f. Summarize the entire unit of work.

3. Require a response
   a. Ask the trainee to provide an overview of the operation, equipment, or workflow.
   b. Ask the trainee to present an overview of the unit of work.
   c. Ask the trainee to tell and show each behavior.
   d. Ask the trainee to explain safety and quality points.
   e. Ask the trainee to summarize of the entire unit of work.

4. Provide feedback
   a. Inform the trainee about the adequacy of responses.
   b. Provide coaching and guidance at points of error.
   c. Point out embedded cues in the work setting.

5. Evaluate performance
   a. Evaluate the trainee's self-report.
   b. Evaluate performance test results.
   c. Document the trainee's performance.

FIGURE 8.1. (*continued*)

have to be secured, and the S-OJT module has to be reviewed. Most of these activities are the responsibility of trainers.

Schedule Training

From the standpoint of supervisors, trainers, and trainees, where and when to conduct the training always seems to pose problems.

Awareness Training

1. Prepare the trainee
   a. Explain the purpose and rationale of the training.
   b. Determine whether the trainee has the prerequisites.
   c. Explain general safety and quality requirements.
   d. Explain how the training will be done.
   e. Ask if trainee has any questions.

2. Present the training
   a. Position the trainee.
   b. Present an overview of the topic or issue.

   Inform
   c. Explain the parts of the topic or issue.
   d. Present examples of the topic or issue.
      (Go to 3c)

   Motivate
   e. Describe the present situation and its consequences.
   f. Describe the desired situation and the associated opportunities.
   g. Present examples of the desired situation.
   h. Describe the implications for individuals and the organization.
   i. Discuss what commitment behaviors would be appropriate.

3. Require a response
   a. Ask the trainee to explain the purpose and rationale of the training.
   b. Ask the trainee to present an overview of the topic or issue.

   Inform
   c. Ask the trainee to explain the parts of the topic or issue.
   d. Ask the trainee to generate examples of the topic or issue.

   Motivate
   e. Ask the trainee to describe the present situation and its consequences.
   f. Ask the trainee to describe the desired situation and the associated opportunities.
   g. Ask the trainee to generate examples of the desired situation.
   h. Ask the trainee to describe the implications for self and others.
   i. Ask the trainee to describe commitment behaviors.

4. Provide feedback
   a. Inform the trainee about the adequacy of responses.
   b. Provide coaching and guidance at points of error.
   c. Point out embedded cues in the work setting.

5. Evaluate performance
   a. Evaluate the trainee's self-report.
   b. Evaluate performance test results.
   c. Document the trainee's performance

FIGURE 8.1. (*continued*)

Training Location

As stated in Chapter 4, the nature of the unit of work can dictate where the training is conducted. S-OJT can sometimes be delivered at the spot where the work is performed—for example, seated before a computer monitor, at the controls of a machine, or at a scheduling board. In other instances, it may not be possible or even necessary to deliver the training where the work is performed.

In the course of identifying the appropriate training location, some organizations have designated areas within the work setting for the delivery of S-OJT. Much like an instructional carrel, these training stations contain all the equipment, information, and resources that one needs to learn the work. These areas are devoted exclusively to S-OJT. They are not for the doing of actual work.

Regardless of where the training occurs, the training location that is selected needs to meet the following criteria:

- Provides the same or nearly the same stimuli and context as the spot where the training does the work

- Does not unduly hinder or inhibit the organization's ongoing production or service delivery activities

- Provides a suitable place in respect to ambient noise, stress, and presence of others who can disrupt the training

Any location that meets these criteria can be suitable. However, the training should not be moved too far away from the spot where the work is done, because that defeats the purpose of using S-OJT in the first place. As emphasized throughout this book, the relevance of the training to the work is one of the primary benefits of using S-OJT. When S-OJT is delivered away from the actual work setting, the trainer may have to follow up after training and observe and coach the trainee in the work setting.

In many organizations, scheduling the S-OJT involves establishing the dates of several training sessions. The training schedule (described in Chapter 7, Table 7.1) includes the titles of the training sessions (or phrases defining the units of work to be learned), the scheduled training dates, the completion dates, and the trainer's approval signature. The training schedule is based on the trainee's development plan.

Training Time

When to deliver the S-OJT is another important issue. The timing of S-OJT depends on the nature of the work and on constraints during the workday. Attempting to squeeze both working and training into the same time period can diminish the effectiveness of both activities. As a result, some organizations have designated formal time periods for the delivery of structure OJT. In this way, line managers and supervisors can know in advance who will be available at certain times of the shift and schedule accordingly. This approach also underlines management's commitment to training as part of the organization's ongoing business.

In many situations, the most effective training times are outside the normal working hours. At those times, trainers are focused on the training, not on other activities. Also, trainers earn extra income by conducting such training. Finally, trainees may feel less pressure, since they are not disrupting ongoing work and do not feel the pressure of having experienced employees watching them perform. If training is conducted during the workday, doing it shortly after the beginning of the work shift is an effective training time. Trainers and trainees are often at their most alert during this time, and it gives trainees time to practice the information presented during the remainder of the shift. It may take only an hour or so for a trainer to present the content, but because some units of work require trainees to practice on their own extensively in order to achieve the training objectives, the entire training session may not be completed until the end of the shift.

Training can also be scheduled as part of planned maintenance activities, which may be the only time in which trainees have access to a particular piece of equipment. In this case, scheduling the delivery of S-OJT may have to be coordinated with maintenance or safety departments.

Secure Training Resources

Making certain that all the training resources required are available and making any other arrangements must also precede the delivery of training. Trainers should take the following steps:

- Arrange for tools, equipment, documents, forms, or any other special resources.
- Inform other employees, managers, or supervisors when the training will be conducted.
- Eliminate any conflicts over the use of resources required for training.
- Schedule a meeting room or work area.

In the broad scheme of organizational priorities, training necessarily ranks lower than work. At the same time, the organization should accommodate requests for training resources. Thus, it is extremely important that both can go on with a minimal amount of conflict. When resource conflicts do occur, more often than not the root cause is the lack of advance planning on the part of the trainer.

Review the Module

The trainer must also review the training content and the various training events before conducting the training. This approach is advised for three reasons. First, the training module may represent areas of knowledge and skills that the

---

TABLE 8.1. Sample Checklist for Getting Ready to Train

Module title: DELEGATING WORK TO EMPLOYEES

SCHEDULE TRAINING	YES	NO
1. Identify training time with trainee	____	____
2. Send trainee's guide to trainee	____	____
3. Schedule conference room	____	____
4. Inform trainee's manager of training time	____	____

SECURE RESOURCES

5. Gather the following resources:	____	____

- Notepad and pencils
- "Delegating Work Vignettes" videotape
- Video player and monitor
- Employee Development Report form

REVIEW MODULE

6. Review contents of module	____	____
7. Review training events in module	____	____
8. Prepare examples for training	____	____
9. Rehearse training delivery	____	____

---

trainer has not used personally for some time. The increased movement toward multiskilling makes this possibility more likely than the reader may initially expect. Second, the content of the module may have changed in some way of which the trainer is not aware. In one memorable instance, the trainer did not review the module beforehand and was confronted with a significant change in safety procedures of which he had no knowledge. HRD staff had revised the training materials as a result of safety concerns expressed by the safety manager.

Finally, the trainer may require some review on how best to present the information to the trainee. For some trainers, review of the module may entail no more than a cursory read-through. For others, review may require a relatively complete rehearsal of the training. The second approach seems important when the work requires the trainee to follow intricate procedures or make complex calculations that may be difficult to replicate each time the training is delivered.

Table 8.1 presents a sample checklist from a S-OJT module. Because the module refers to managerial training, the training can be conducted in a conference room instead of the actual work setting. The module referred to in this checklist uses a video program in conjunction with the one-on-one training.

CONCLUSION

Five training events are used to deliver S-OJT. The exact nature of the events differs for each type of training. The training events increase the chances that trainees will achieve the training objectives. Before delivering S-OJT, a trainer should perform three basic activities in order to get ready: schedule the training, secure training resources, and review the training module.

Chapter 9
Delivering Managerial, Technical, and Awareness Training

The primary focus in this chapter is how the trainer actually delivers the training. To achieve the intended training objectives, trainers should use the five training events discussed in Chapter 8 to deliver the S-OJT. Instrumental in this chapter is the following question:

- How is each training event delivered for the different types of training?

DELIVERING STRUCTURED ON-THE-JOB TRAINING

This chapter focuses on the delivery of S-OJT. This information is presented prescriptively, because the reader should have a complete understanding of this process. Nevertheless, given the importance of training events, trainers should develop their own individual styles into training delivery. Thus, the reader should not consider this account representative of the one best way of delivering S-OJT.

For example, some experienced trainers have learned to alter the sequence of events or vary the emphasis placed on individual events in order to accommodate the needs of particular trainees. Others have learned how to blend the middle three training events—presentation, response, and feedback—into a seamless, repeating cycle of trainer behavior. Such a blending helps make the training session like an easygoing but still purposeful social interaction between two individuals, not a stiff formal presentation. It should be emphasized that one moves toward such a level of trainer ability only with a thorough prior understanding of the training events.

Finally, trainers must use effective communication skills. From the beginning of the training session, the trainer should maintain eye contact with the trainee, speak clearly and distinctly, use humor appropriately and only when related to the training, and display positive nonverbal messages. Any trainer should have learned these skills as part of his or her own training and development program.

1. PREPARE THE TRAINEE

As Table 9.1 shows, trainers should do the same basic five actions for all three types of training. In practice, this training event can occur immediately before the training, a few hours before the training, or even a few days before the training. Sometimes, this training event takes place well before the S-OJT so that the trainee has plenty of time to review the training module. When this training event occurs often depends on the complexity or the difficulty of the work to be learned.

In preparing the trainee, the trainer should first explain the purpose and rationale of the training. Often a rhetorical question helps the trainer begin to make the point:

"Have you ever wanted to know what to do when the parts were out of tolerance? Making certain that we

TABLE 9.1. Prepare the Trainee		
Managerial	*Technical*	*Awareness*
	a. Explain the purpose and rationale of the training.	
	b. Determine whether the trainee has the prerequisites.	
	c. Explain general safety and quality requirements.	
	d. Explain how the training will be done.	
	e. Ask whether trainee has any questions.	

send out only good parts is an important part of the operator's job. Our customers depend on the quality of our parts. Well, that's the purpose of this training program. This training program will help you troubleshoot part problems."

Presenting the purpose and rationale in this way, regardless of the type of training involved, helps the trainer gain the trainee's attention, and it helps the trainee anticipate what will be presented during the training. It also helps the trainee begin to understand the performance expected as a result of the training. The trainer's comments concerning the rationale should link the training with work and organizational outcomes.

Because learning even the simplest unit of work or information requires the trainee to possess some prerequisite knowledge and skills, the next step is for the trainer to verify that the trainee has the necessary prerequisites. The trainer can examine firsthand records of the trainee's past training and work experiences before training begins, or the trainer can now ask the trainee selected questions, the answers to which indicate the trainee's level of knowledge and skills. If the trainee does not have all or some of the prerequisites, the trainer can either suspend the training or alter the point at which the training begins in order to accommodate the trainee's entering level of knowledge and skills. Prerequisite knowledge and skills are often more critical for technical and managerial training than they are for awareness training.

Next, the trainer reviews the general safety and quality requirements of the training. In most situations, two levels of safety and quality requirements can be identified: general safety and quality information related to the work and specific safety and quality information. For example, the trainer should review the basic safety measures associated with working in a certain area (e.g., wear goggles or special gloves) or performing an operation (e.g., follow the accepted lockout procedures). Quality information can include such things as a review of the company's quality philosophy or the customer's requirements—for example:

"Remember, we don't pass bad parts on to anyone."

"We expect new supervisors to perform all the steps of the appraisal process."

The next step in preparing the trainee is to explain how the training will be done. The trainer outlines the steps that will be followed in general terms. The explanation can be as simple as:

"First, I will show you how to do it, then I will ask you to repeat the steps back to me. Do you understand?"

Last, answering any questions that the trainee may have can help increase the training's effectiveness. You may even want to prompt trainees to ask questions about the training. It is common for trainees to display signs of anxiety. They may be fearful of appearing incompetent in front of others, especially if the other person has higher status within the organization. The trainer should spend whatever time it takes to put the trainee at ease about the challenges in learning the content. The following suggestions can help the trainer loosen up the situation:

- Make an effort to learn some personal information about the trainee—for example, outside interests, past work experiences, friends in common.
- Begin the training session by introducing yourself, asking the trainee to do the same, and following up with some small talk.
- Show enthusiasm for the training and the interesting aspects of the work.
- Remark that other trainees have felt anxious about training and that they were able to overcome their feelings and be successful in learning the information.

2. PRESENT THE TRAINING

As shown in Table 9.2, the actions associated with the second training event differ markedly as a result of the type of training being delivered.

Managerial Training
The first step is to position the trainee. The arrangement of trainer and trainee necessarily differs from that in technical training. In managerial training, trainer and trainee usually sit facing each other. The arrangement resembles a conversation much more than it does a demonstration. The trainer may have to indicate explicitly to the trainee where it is best to sit.

Next, the trainer presents an overview of the model or process that defines the unit of work. As stated, managerial training generally requires the trainee first to learn about a model or process, then to learn specific techniques used to apply the model or process. Suppose, for example, that new

TABLE 9.2. Present the Training

Managerial	Technical	Awareness
a. Position the trainee.	a. Position the trainee.	a. Position the trainee.
b. Present an overview of the model, process, or project.	b. Present an overview of the operation, equipment, or workflow.	b. Present an overview of the topic or issue.
c. Present examples of the model, process, or project.	c. Present an overview of the unit of work.	*Inform* c. Explain the parts of the topic or issue.
d. Explain parts of the model, process, or project.	d. Tell and show each behavior.	d. Present examples of the topic or issue. (Go to 3c)
e. Explain techniques to apply the model, process, or project.	e. Explain specific safety and quality points.	*Motivate*
f. Demonstrate techniques to apply the model, process, or project.	f. Summarize the entire unit of work.	e. Describe the present situation and its consequences.
g. Summarize the entire model, process, or project.		f. Describe the desired situation and the associated opportunities.
		g. Present examples of the desired situation.
		h. Describe the implications for individuals and the organization.
		i. Discuss what commitment behaviors would be appropriate.

supervisors are being trained on the grievance process. The trainer can begin by saying:

"Here are the steps of the grievance process that we use here. The process starts at this point, and ends with a successful resolution at this point. All of us work together to make sure employee issues are fairly addressed."

For a conceptual model, the trainer could say:

"This model shows the relationship between supervisory feedback and employee performance. We believe that appropriate and timely feedback from supervisors can influence how people do their jobs. Have you ever thought that you could influence others in this way?"

At some point, the trainer would present relevant positive and negative examples of the work. This information can be given before or after the parts of the model or process are presented. A trainer has some discretion in determining the sequence of training actions. In some training situations, the trainer might want to begin by asking the trainee to come up with an example:

"Tell me about the feedback that you have received on your first job. Did you think it was adequate at the time? What was lacking from it?"

Then, the trainer explains the individual parts of the model or process, one by one. Understanding specific parts of the model or process can help the trainee understand the concepts involved in the work. Those who have written on concept learning, especially Tiemann and Markle (1983), can provide further help in this regard.

Next, the trainer introduces the techniques related to the concepts, often in the form of chains of verbal information. Knowledge of a model or process is not very useful if the trainee cannot do something with it. For example, one part of a grievance process that concerns a supervisor is handling conflicts between employees locally before they can become larger and expensive issues. Knowledge of the grievance process and of conflict resolution techniques can be considered a single unit of work.

Logically, the trainer's next action is to demonstrate the techniques, using an established set of behaviors. In contrast to technical training, which often requires a trainee to reproduce the behavior exactly as demonstrated, managerial training can accept different behaviors, depending on the individual preferences and experiences of trainers and trainees. But the same criteria should be met no matter what behaviors are used.

Role plays can be extremely effective in demonstrating certain managerial behaviors. For instance, videotaped scenarios derived from critical incidents have been used (Jacobs, 1986). The trainer should make sure to point out critical aspects shown during the scenarios.

The last step is for the trainer to summarize the training content in its entirety.

Technical Training

Most technical training requires the trainer to demonstrate a set of behavioral actions to the trainee. Thus, the trainer's first action—positioning the trainee to receive the training—is critical. In doing so, the trainer may literally have to walk the trainee to the location at which the training will be conducted. Once they have reached the training location, the trainer may have to guide the trainee physically into the most appropriate position.

For example, to ensure proper positioning, the trainer may have to take hold of the trainee's hands and show the trainee exactly how to hold a tool. The trainer should always make certain that the intent of the action is clear before he or she touches the trainee.

To observe a demonstration, the trainee should be positioned to the side or slightly to the rear of the trainer. In this way, the trainee can view the demonstration from the perspective in which the trainer conducts it. If the trainee is positioned directly in front of the trainer, he or she has a mirror image, which requires the trainee to interpret the trainer's actions, translate right into left, and so on. Finally, the trainer should avoid placing physical barriers between himself or herself and the trainee. Proper positioning helps to reduce unnecessary hindrances on the trainee's ability to learn. It can be encouraged by statements such as:

> "I am going to move you right here so that you can see what I'm doing from a better angle. Don't stand over there, or you won't be able to see everything."

Next, the trainer provides an overview of the operation, piece of equipment, or system workflow in which the unit of work is embedded. The overview specifies where the work comes from, what actions are done at this stage, and who receives the products or services that result from this stage. This information provides a context for the training content that will follow—for example:

> "As you may know, when the forms get to us, the pricing information for each item has been included on the contract. Our job here is to make sure that all the prices meet our profit requirements. After we're done with the contract, it goes on to sales, where they send it to the customer."

At this point, the trainer can describe and show individual behaviors one at a time. During the presentation, the trainee should observe the trainer and, if possible, follow along in the training module. The trainer should always describe the behavior first, often by reading it from the training module or having the trainee read what it says. Only then should the trainer demonstrate the behavior. Saying, then doing, helps reinforce the content for the trainee, pace the trainer's disclosure of content, and ensure that key points can be highlighted before the action is taken. The trainer should be prepared to repeat a behavior several times.

As each behavior is presented, the trainer explains any specific quality and safety points associated with it. It is critical for this information to be included in the training module. The trainer should be able to present the behavior and associated quality and safety points as one complete chunk of information.

After presenting all the behaviors, the trainer summarizes the entire unit of work or at least the complete chain of behaviors presented in the demonstration. Most often, this summary is oral. The summary helps the trainee link the separate behaviors of the task into a meaningful, complete whole. Such linking is especially necessary if the task is complex and lengthy and if it has to be learned in small bits.

Awareness Training

As in managerial training, the trainer positions the trainee in awareness training as if the two were engaged in conversation. If the awareness training is meant to inform the trainee about information, the trainer should provide an overview of the topic, then cover each of the specific parts of the topic in detail. Here's an example:

> "This package contains all the information about our profit-sharing plan. There are several details we will cover today, so that you will know how you will be compensated. Let's begin with the first point. . . ."

If the awareness training is meant to inform the trainee about an idea, concept, or issue, then the trainer should explain each of its component parts. Relevant examples are often extremely important in awareness training.

When the awareness training is meant to motivate the trainee to form an opinion about something, the trainer approaches the training differently. The trainer begins by describing the present condition in some detail and follows up with examples that make the present condition concrete. The trainer may ask the trainee to copy down some of the ideas articulated during the presentation.

Next, the trainer describes the consequences of the present condition—for example:

"As you know just by looking around, when we produce a lot of parts at one time, we also make a lot of bad ones. Defects cost the company a lot of money. In the long run, it takes money out of all our pockets. Just last month, when we did the large order for Acme Company, we had over $20,000 in rework costs that could have been avoided."

Next, the trainer describes the desired condition in some depth and the opportunities that the desired condition can offer. It may be necessary to provide additional examples that help the trainee to understand the desired condition. If the information is new to the organization, the examples may have to come from other settings. Then, the trainer discusses the implications for individuals and the organization by moving toward the desired condition. The sequence gives the trainee a basis from which to understand the what, why, and how of the information being presented. Throughout this part of the presentation, the trainer should make sure to present the implications in a fair and objective manner.

Finally, it is important for the trainer to discuss what is required of the trainee in order to make the change occur. This helps identify the specific behaviors that demonstrate the trainee's commitment to change. Some trainers have used a modified version of the force-field analysis technique at this time, as described by Zemke and Kramlinger (1984), to identify the issues that may hinder commitment.

Here is a training sequence used when supervisors were asked to help front-line workers become aware of the organization's change from a push to a pull production system: Supervisors delivered the S-OJT to three to four trainees at a time. Each production approach was introduced, and the consequences of the two approaches were discussed. Soon, in spite of the general conclusion that the pull system would require employees to work harder, employees became comfortable with the change, primarily because they understood what it was and why it was being used

3. REQUIRE A RESPONSE

Whenever training is presented, trainees must have opportunities to respond actively. As Table 9.3 shows, managerial, technical, and awareness types of training require different types of responses.

Managerial Training

In managerial training, when the trainer prompts the trainer to respond, he or she asks the trainee to repeat the purpose and rationale of the training. Then, the trainer asks the trainee to explain the model or process. Next, the trainer asks the trainee either to give some examples of how the model or process is used or to respond to examples that were presented during the training.

The trainer expects the trainee to state why specific examples do or do not fit the concept defined during training. For example, the trainer can introduce a subordinate feedback model that lacks at least one critical attribute. The trainee should be able to identify the missing attribute and state the consequences that its absence can have on a subordinate's performance. Then, the trainee should explain the parts of the model or process in a meaningful way.

Possibly the most important aspect of the trainee's responses is his or her ability to demonstrate that he or she

TABLE 9.3. Require a Response

Managerial	*Technical*	*Awareness*
a. Ask the trainee to present an overview of the model, process, or project. b. Ask the trainee for examples of the model, process, or project. c. Ask the trainee to explain parts of the model, process, or project. d. Ask the trainee to explain techniques to apply the model, process, or project. e. Ask the trainee to demonstrate techniques to apply the model, process, or project. f. Ask the trainee to summarize the entire model, process, or project.	a. Ask the trainee to provide an overview of the operation, equipment, or workflow. b. Ask the trainee to present an overview of the unit of work. c. Ask the trainee to tell and show each behavior. d. Ask the trainee to explain safety and quality points. e. Ask the trainee to summarize the entire unit of work.	a. Ask the trainee to explain the purpose and rationale of the training. b. Ask the trainee to present an overview of the topic or issue. *Inform* c. Ask the trainee to explain the parts of the topic or issue. d. Ask the trainee to generate examples of the topic or issue. *Motivate* e. Ask the trainee to describe the present situation and its consequences. f. Ask the trainee to describe the desired situation and the associated opportunities. g. Ask the trainee to generate examples of the desired situation. h. Ask the trainee to describe the implications for self and others. i. Ask the trainee to describe commitment behaviors.

can use the related techniques appropriately. To this end, the trainer can suggest that they engage in a role-play situation in which the trainer must be certain to elicit all possible variations of the desired responses from the trainee.

Finally, the trainer asks the trainee to summarize the entire unit of work.

Technical Training

Presumably, the opportunity to observe the trainer explain and demonstrate the work prepares the trainee to explain and demonstrate the same work. The trainer usually begins by prompting the trainee—for example:

> "OK, now it's your turn to show me. I want you to tell me the purpose of the task and why it is important. Then, I want you to tell and show me how to do each step, including all the quality and safety points along the way."

The trainer should also tell the trainee to what extent he or she can use the training module during the response. In most instances, the trainee should be able to use the module whenever required, since it was not intended for the trainee to memorize its content. Throughout the trainee's response, the trainer prompts the trainee to respond in specific ways determined by the training objective. It may be necessary to have the trainee restate the general safety and quality requirements of the work at this time.

For several reasons, it is important to have the trainee first describe, then perform the response. First, such a sequence allows the trainer to step in if the trainee proposes to perform an action that is unsafe or that would have harmful consequences. Also, such a sequence may reinforce the content since it calls on two independent response modes. Finally, because some responses may have to be verbal only—for example, describing the removal of a part that cannot be touched—trainers always have at least one way of determining whether the trainee has learned the content.

Depending on the size of the unit of work, the trainer may not wait until all the training content has been presented. Instead, the trainer may decide to separate the content into logical chunks and require the trainee to respond at the end of each chunk. Within the context of the response, the trainee includes the safety and quality information related to the particular chunk. Finally, the trainer may want to have the trainee link the various parts of the content into one continuous response set. Often, this linking can be done orally.

Awareness Training

For both forms of awareness training, the trainee's response requirements are relatively straightforward. The trainee should provide a brief overview of the topic and then describe each part of the topic. It may be necessary to have the trainee conclude by summarizing the content of the training. The trainer should encourage the trainee to use words that are most meaningful to him or her.

When awareness training is used to inform, the trainee should be required first to explain the topic or issue in his or her own words, then to give original examples of the topic of training. When awareness training is used to motivate trainees to form an opinion, the response requirements are necessarily more involved. In the appropriate wording, the trainee should be asked first to describe the present condition, then to discuss some consequences of the present condition in depth. Next, the trainee should be asked to produce some examples of the desired condition. Finally, the trainer should ask the trainee to discuss the implications of the desired condition for the trainee, for other employees in the trainee's work areas, and perhaps also for the organization as a whole.

In this way, trainer and trainee can begin to discuss the actions that the trainee should take to achieve the desired condition. After the trainee has stated the value of the desired condition and reconciled the implications, the trainer should attempt to obtain statements that the trainee is committed to achieving the desired condition.

The trainer should not try to coerce the trainee into making statements that are harmful or counter to the trainee's actual beliefs. Rather, the statement of commitment helps to bind the trainee to the new ideas, and it suggests behaviors that the trainee can take in accordance with the commitment.

4. PROVIDE FEEDBACK

As Table 9.4 shows, all three types of training require the same basic actions from the trainer. The trainer should give feedback based on an objective assessment of the adequacy of the trainee's response. The behavior sciences literature has well documented the potency of feedback on learning. Feedback has been shown to have even greater impact when the persons involved have differing levels of status. The relationship between trainer and trainee often entails such a status differential, which can be based on differences in formal job roles or simply on the respect that people tend to

TABLE 9.4. Provide Feedback		
Managerial	*Technical*	*Awareness*
	a. Inform the trainee about the adequacy of responses. b. Provide coaching and guidance at points of error. c. Point out embedded cues in the work setting.	

give to those who have demonstrated high levels of competence in a particular topic.

The first step of this training event is to inform the trainee about the correctness of his or her response. The feedback should be given immediately or very soon after the response. Unless the trainee's response involves harmful consequences, the trainer should refrain from giving feedback while the trainee responds. Interrupting a response can deform it and diminish the trainee's sense of achievement. There is no standard way of phrasing or delivering feedback, but the trainer should strive to be specific about the elements of the response that were correct and the elements that were not correct. Effective feedback does not always need to be positive.

The next step of this training event is to provide coaching and learning guidance when appropriate. If a large number of the trainee's responses are incorrect and it is obvious that the trainee cannot possibly make correct responses on his or her own, then the trainer may have to repeat the training, this time reducing the size of the individual chunks of the training content. The trainee can be expected to respond at the conclusion of each chunk. However, if the trainee makes a few incorrect responses or if the errors are concentrated in a few areas, the trainer can elect to coach the trainee in order to achieve the correct responses (Fournies, 1978). That is, the trainer provides a continuous set of behavioral prompts focused on relatively small parts of the training content, and the trainee responds immediately.

While it is important for the trainer to provide the trainee with feedback and coaching, not all the feedback should come from the trainer. The trainer should help trainees identify independent sources of feedback embedded in the work itself. For some tasks, such as making an adjustment to the height of a press ram or using a sales technique on a prospective buyer, the feedback is automatic. In both of the cases just cited, the trainee can observe the immediate outcome of these actions, which in effect are independent sources of feedback. For that reason, the trainer should include in his or her feedback information about where the trainee can look for feedback on his or her own. Feedback is often more effective when it comes from sources that tell the trainee directly whether his or her response is correct without necessarily involving others.

5. EVALUATE PERFORMANCE

As Table 9.5 shows, the fifth training event requires the trainer to use trainee self-reports and objective performance tests to determine whether the trainee has in fact achieved the intended training objectives. The trainer considers the information available, then documents the decision in the trainee's development plan or similar personnel record.

The term trainee *self-report* refers to the trainee's own evaluation of his or her learning progress. To gather such information, the trainer should ask the trainee to reflect critically on what he or she has accomplished and on the areas in which he or she may require additional practice. A trainer should not be coy. For example, the trainer can ask directly:

> "Do you feel that you have achieved the objective? Do you think you can now perform the task on your own? What areas of the task are still unclear to you?"

In interpreting a trainee's self-evaluation, the trainer may wonder whether the trainee is giving an honest opinion or merely a response that he or she believes to be socially acceptable. After all, the trainee may not want to disappoint the trainer, regardless of the truth of the matter. Nevertheless, research tends to support the notion that adults can and will assess their own learning progress accurately, even if the assessment is to their disadvantage. Recent studies on self-directed learning have shown that adults are capable of

TABLE 9.5. Evaluate Performance		
Managerial	*Technical*	*Awareness*
	a. Evaluate the trainee's self-report.	
	b. Evaluate performance test results.	
	c. Document the trainee's performance.	

wisely selecting learning activities to address internal and external development needs. Moreover, studies on learner-controlled instruction conducted during the 1960s and 1970s found no significant differences in achievement between trainees who were permitted to skip over content that self-assessment indicated they had already learned and trainees who were required to complete all content.

The term *performance test* refers to the trainer's judgment of the adequacy of the trainee's responses. The trainer bases the judgment on standards that refer to the training objective. To gather this information, the trainer uses performance rating scales or cognitive tests. Performance rating scales require a trainer to observe the trainee's actions or the result of the actions and then give a partial and an overall rating.

Cognitive tests, such as multiple-choice and completion tests, can also help the trainer to evaluate the trainee's performance. In practice, cognitive tests are limited in their ability to measure work performance and thus are less useful than performance-rating scales for most S-OJT situations. Cognitive tests can be useful in testing the attainment of concepts and principles associated with awareness training.

The issues of reliability and validity invariably arise whenever a trainer evaluates a trainee. In relative terms, validity—that is, whether the test actually measures what was presented—is of less concern than reliability, since the high relevance of S-OJT ensures that the training objectives match work expectations. However, reliability raises two basic questions. First, would two or more trainers evaluate similar behaviors in the same way? Second, would the same trainer evaluate similar behaviors in different trainees in the same way? These two questions can be addressed through a thorough training and development program for trainers and through ongoing monitoring of the trainers.

Finally, the trainer completes the training by reaching a summative judgment about the trainee's performance. This judgment is based on the self-reports and performance tests. As stated, this information documents that the trainee has completed the training. In an increasing number of organizations, the trainer's evaluation leads to a formal certification for the employee in doing the unit of work.

CONCLUSION

This chapter has shown how to deliver S-OJT for the three types of training. The five training events provide the time-tested method for ensuring effective training. In practice, S-OJT seldom occurs in the same way for every trainee. Some trainees require relatively small chunks of content before responding, while others can handle large chunks. The trainer makes the judgment while delivering the training. Training seldom occurs in a straight, linear path. Usually, some steps need to be repeated.

Chapter 10

Evaluating and Troubleshooting Structured On-the-Job Training Programs

The last step of the S-OJT process is to evaluate and troubleshoot the training. Of course, in a practical sense, evaluating and troubleshooting are continuous, ongoing activities in any system. This chapter presents the following topics:

- Questions that should be asked to evaluate S-OJT
- Ways to troubleshoot training system components and issues arising from the organizational context

EVALUATION QUESTIONS

Several authors (e.g., Russ-Eft & Preskill, 2001; Robinson & Robinson, 1998; Brinkerhoff, 1987) have addressed the evaluation of human resource development activities. This chapter focuses on the questions used to evaluate S-OJT. The S-OJT system that was introduced in Chapter 2 provides a framework specific for organizing the questions. That is, the questions that should be asked are based on the system components of outcomes, processes, and inputs. Questions should also be asked about the organizational system in which the training system resides.

Figure 10.1 presents a list of questions related to system components and organizational context. It is common in evaluation to establish desired performance standards for each question and then to compare actual performance with standards. In that way, the value and worth of each component and of the entire system as a whole can be determined. An evaluation that asks these questions will be conducted by a team of employees who are knowledgeable in the use of evaluation methods, perhaps with assistance from outside consultants.

The remainder of this section discusses the evaluation questions outlined in Figure 10.1. Where appropriate, additional information from experience is provided. The discussion begins with training outputs, since these are often most critical when evaluating systems. It makes no sense to ask, say, whether the training was conducted properly if the training objectives had been met. In a truly effective system, both questions should be answered affirmatively.

Training Output Questions

Training output questions focus on the various effects of having used S-OJT. These questions look at what is left over after the training has been completed. The following are some possible areas of focus of output questions:

- Training objectives
- Trainee's development goals
- Organizational goals
- Unanticipated effects

Training output questions usually raise the most interest among system stakeholders. Simply put, if a senior manager wants proof that a S-OJT program works, the output questions provide the basis for a response.

Training Outputs

1. Were the training objectives achieved?
2. What were the effects on organizational performance?
3. What were the effects on training effectiveness?
4. What were the effects on training efficiency?
5. Were the training outcomes consistent with the trainee's development needs?
6. Were there any unanticipated effects?

Training Process

1. How much time did it take to conduct the training?
2. Was the training location adequate?
3. Were the needed resources available?
4. Did the trainer get ready to train?
5. Did the trainer use the module as intended?
6. Did the trainer use the training events as intended?
7. Was the communications technology used appropriately?
8. Did the trainer document the training as intended?
9. Did the trainee use the module as instructed?
10. Did the trainee attend to the trainer?
11. Did the trainee ask questions? What kind of questions?
12. Did the trainee like the training content?
13. Did the trainee like the training approach?

Training Inputs

1. Was the unit of work appropriate for S-OJT?
2. Was the unit of work analyzed adequately?
3. Was the module accurate, complete, and clear?
4. Was the training design appropriate?
5. Were the resources available in the training setting?
6. Was the training setting suitable for the delivery of S-OJT?
7. Was the communications technology suitable for S-OJT?
8. Did the trainee have the prerequisites for training?
9. Did the trainee have the personality or learning style suitable for S-OJT?
10. Was the most appropriate experienced employee selected as trainer?
11. Did the experienced employee receive adequate training and development experiences?

Organizational Context

1. Did management provide sufficient resources to support S-OJT?
2. Can S-OJT occur within the constraints of the ongoing production or service delivery?
3. Do labor–management contractual agreements allow employees to participate as trainers?
4. Are staffing levels sufficient to allow experienced employees to take time to train others?
5. Is the organizational culture consistent with S-OJT?
6. Are there external issues ongoing inhibit the use of S-OJT?

FIGURE 10.1. S-OJT Evaluation Questions

The training output question that is usually asked first is whether the training objectives have been met. As stated in Chapter 9, the trainer's use of performance-rating scales and cognitive tests does much to address this evaluation question in the short term. In the long term, this question can be addressed by interviewing trainees at specified intervals after training, by interviewing supervisors, or by reviewing performance records. Given the planned nature of S-OJT, it is highly likely that the intended training objectives will be achieved.

Of note, the U.S. Department of Energy guidelines for using S-OJT in nuclear power facilities mandates that the OJT have two phases: training and evaluation. Thus, the trainer would be responsible for delivering the training only, while another person, such as a supervisor, would be responsible for observing the trainee and evaluating his or her performance of the task after the training (Kluch & Whatley, 2002). Separating the training program delivery from the training program evaluation helps ensure an independent judgment of the trainee's ability to perform the work.

It may also be important to determine whether training objectives were consistent with the trainees' development goals. While it is important to show that S-OJT achieves the training objectives, it may also be equally important to determine whether the training met the needs of trainees. For a training program to be truly effective, it should be viewed as a means to achieve organizational and individual goals. However, the individual goals have to be expressed beforehand, and they have to be articulated with the needs of the organization.

For most managers, the bottom line in S-OJT is its effect on the effort to achieve business goals. Training objectives should be linked with measures of work or group performance during the analysis that precedes the design of S-OJT. The business goals are the reason for conducting the training in the first place. Unfortunately, while this bottom-line aspect of training evaluation has generated much interest and attracted attention, for a variety of reasons it is seldom addressed in organizations. A few notable exceptions exist, such as a study of OJT and work performance measures by Kainen, Begley, and Maggard (1983).

Two questions seem important to managers when comparing the effects of S-OJT, unstructured OJT, and classroom-based training. The financial forecasting models and related tools that allow bottom-line evaluations to be achieved with a high degree of confidence can be found in the literature (Swanson, 2001).

Studies on S-OJT have focused on two basic questions: first, whether the outcomes of S-OJT, unstructured OJT, and classroom training differ in their effectiveness.

> Do employees who receive S-OJT perform work better than employees who receive another kind of training?

Second is whether one kind of training is more efficient than the other.

> Does S-OJT achieve the objectives faster than other training approaches and, if it does, what are the financial implications?

The performance time graph shown in Figure 10.2 has helped guide thinking on the first question. The vertical axis shows the level of competence—from the novice to the specialist level. Based on the discussion in Chapter 1, trainees should achieve the specialist level through training. That is, because of their limited practice and experience with the unit of work, they cannot handle more than the routine instances of the unit of work. The horizontal axis shows the passage of time to achieve the specialist level. The longer dotted line represents the learning time for unstructured OJT. The shorter solid line represents the learning time for S-OJT. The difference between the two learning times—unstructured OJT versus S-OJT—is represented as savings in

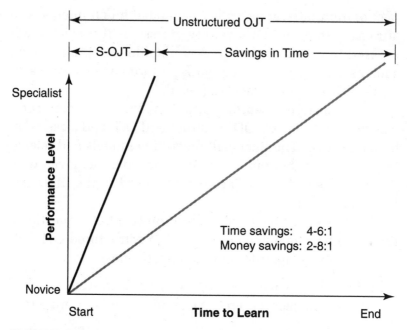

FIGURE 10.2. Comparing the Training Efficiency of S-OJT and Unstructured OJT

time. The basic question is this: Does it make good economic sense to invest in S-OJT as opposed to other forms of training, such as unstructured OJT, even though the costs of S-OJT are higher?

Studies consistently show that S-OJT is superior to unstructured OJT in training situations in which a performance need has been demonstrated. Considering a range of organizations and differing units of work, the following have been concluded about the relationship between unstructured and structured OJT: S-OJT requires between four to six times less time than unstructured OJT. S-OJT represents between two to eight times financial benefits compared to unstructured OJT.

As Figure 10.3 shows, comparisons of training effectiveness have sought to address the second evaluation question. Studies have shown that employees who learn work through

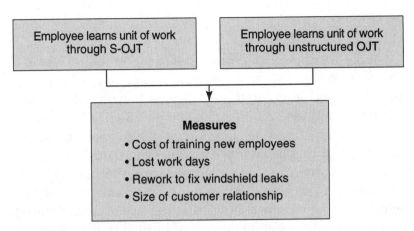

FIGURE 10.3. Comparing the Training Effectiveness of S-OJT and Unstructured OJT

S-OJT have a lower cost of training, have fewer lost workdays, make lower rework costs, and have a greater relationship with customers than employees who learn through unstructured OJT. These outcomes have had a substantial financial impact on organizations. For example, the financial benefits of reducing the quality errors for a single assembly task over one year have been calculated at $24,000 (Jacobs, 1994).

In addition, employees achieve training objectives faster and more completely through S-OJT than unstructured OJT. The increased efficiency and thoroughness have been shown to have financial benefits. For example, an organization that increased training efficiency by a factor of five times through S-OJT received twice the financial benefits in terms of employee productivity (Jacobs et al., 1992).

Readers should address similar questions whenever possible in their own organizations. The techniques may seem complicated, or the data required to conduct the analyses may be difficult to obtain. Despite the challenges involved, however, the results can have important payoffs. Few other evaluation questions have the same degree of relevance and meaning for an organization's leaders and managers when you have to justify the use of S-OJT.

Table 10.1 presents a form used to report the results of a financial analysis to management. In this particular example, the report forecasted the financial benefits of unstructured OJT, a three-day off-site class, and S-OJT. The unit of work was how first-line supervisors should coach others to use proper lifting behaviors. Of note, even though the training was planned for thirty supervisors, the performance measure is taken from injury rates incurred among front-line employees. The report shows that the use of unstructured OJT resulted in a $96,000 financial burden to the organization. The use of a three-day off-site class was forecasted to reduce the burden to $51,000. The use of S-OJT was forecasted to reduce the burden to $21,000. Thus, the calculation shows that for every training dollar invested in S-OJT, the organization could realize a savings of $75,000 compared to unstructured OJT and $45,000 compared to the three-day off-site training.

Finally, S-OJT can have unanticipated effects, both positive and negative. For example, the following outcomes have been observed regarding S-OJT:

- Empowers employees to become part of the ongoing activities of their work areas. Employees come to have a greater stake in the outcomes that are produced by all.

- Increases the perception among employees that the organization cares about their progress and that it is willing to commit scarce resources to this end.

- Removes some of the fears and anxieties that employees have about learning new information. Learning should not be a test. Rather, learning should be made as easy as possible.

- Provides managers a means of observing promising front-line employees and assessing them for possible

TABLE 10.1. Example S-OJT Financial Analysis Report

Organization: Electric Utility Company
Unit of Work: Coach safe lifting behaviors
Trainees: First-line supervisors

	TRAINING OPTIONS		
	Unstructured OJT	*Three-Day Class*	*S-OJT*
Unit of measure	Back injuries among front-line employees		
Current performance	24 injuries per year		
Desired performance	0 injuries per year	0 injuries per year	0 injuries per year
Cost per back injury per one year	$4,000 × 24 = $96,000	$ 0	$ 0
Number of participants	30	30	30
Training cost	$0	Wages per day $500 × 3 days × 30 participants = $45,000 Training design and delivery $200 × 30 participants = $6,000 Total training cost = $51,000	Wages per day $500 × 1 day × 30 participants = $15,000 Training design and delivery $200 × 30 participants = $6,000 Total training cost = $21,000
Financial burden/ opportunity	$96,000	$51,000	$21,000
Savings compared to unstructured OJT		$45,000 savings	$75,000 savings

promotion. It requires employees to accept responsibility and authority, and fosters self-direction and confidence. How individual employees respond to these challenges are important to management.

- Distributes the responsibility for the development of appropriate competence throughout the organization while maintaining that the ultimate accountability lies with management and the individual employee.

- Becomes part of the organization's ongoing continuous improvement efforts, since the training outcomes are being scrutinized by those who actually do the work.

- Increases discussion among all employees about the one best way of doing something and diminishes the variations in individual practice. It requires employees to begin to reflect on how they do their work.

- Provides the HRD staff a distinct role. Before S-OJT is introduced, it seems likely that their influence on how OJT was conducted within the organization was limited. HRD staff should help to design and manage S-OJT.

- Increases the transfer of specific work information between departments, such as between engineering and production, and between locations at which similar work is being done.

- Ensures that everyone is being trained to do the work in the same way. Standardization of work practices becomes a basis for certifying employees to perform jobs in compliance with ISO 9000 requirements.

- Provides a basis for establishing high standards in doing the work. The same criteria can be applied to all employees.

Jacobs and Hruby-Moore (1998) report the unanticipated effect of a negative financial analysis in using S-OJT after a positive financial analysis has been originally forecasted in the organization. Such a result for a cost–benefit analysis is rarely noted in the literature, but the intent is to show what happens when management follow-through does not occur to the extent promised at the beginning of the project.

Training Process Questions

Training process questions focus on the behaviors of trainer and trainee during the training. They ask how the S-OJT was carried out and how the content was learned. While process questions may have less interest for managers than output questions, they provide valuable insights into the workings of training. Answering process questions usually requires observation during training and interviews after training. To ensure that the observational data that are gathered are consistent, standardized forms that measure the frequency of the trainer's and trainee's behaviors need to be developed. Appendix B shows the form used to observe to the performance of S-OJT trainers.

The general questions about the training process address such issues as the amount of time required to complete training. It is also important to know whether the training resources needed for training were in fact available for use during training. Finally, questions can be asked about the suitability of the work setting to the delivery of training.

Evaluation questions about the trainer's behavior ask whether the trainer did all that was necessary to get ready for training, how the trainer used the training module and the training events, and whether the trainer followed by completing all ratings and personnel forms as expected. Whether the trainer effectively used communications skills should also be questioned.

While learning occurs within individuals, inferences can be made about learning progress by observing outward behaviors. The process questions about the trainee's behavior ask whether the trainee used the module as instructed by the trainer. How the trainee responded to the trainer during the training should be observed. What kind of questions were asked during the training should be noted. Finally, how the trainees felt about the content and process of S-OJT should be noted. Appendix C shows the form used to allow trainees to rate their trainer's performance during the training.

Some people downplay the role of attitudes and feelings, but at the very least, knowing how a trainee feels about his or her training process can help an organization chart that trainee's later course of action.

Training Input Questions

Training input questions focus on the system components present at the time of the training: unit of work to be learned, the training module, training location in the work setting, the trainee, and the trainer. As explained in the next section of this chapter, many if not all problems associated with the use of S-OJT can be traced back to the absence of some input component. Answering evaluation questions about training input usually requires us to conduct interviews.

Questions about the unit of work to be learned ask whether it was appropriate for S-OJT and whether it was analyzed adequately. While the training module and the training design that it reflects are clearly system inputs, it may be possible to gather information about them by asking questions about the process. For example, determining whether the module format was appropriate or the training sequence was logical may depend on obtaining information from the trainee and trainer during training.

Questions about the work setting focus on the availability of training resources and the overall suitability of the work setting as a training location. Many issues about the use of the work setting for training should have been resolved when the training location was selected. However, it is reasonable to assume that all issues cannot be anticipated and that it is therefore appropriate to ask such questions after training as well.

The amount of time invested in evaluation questions about the trainee and trainer can depend on the effectiveness of prior planning activities. Clearly, it is not appropriate to allow a trainee who lacks the prerequisites or the personality required for training to attend training. It is also not appropriate to allow an inexperienced employee or an employee who has not received adequate training and development experiences beforehand to conduct the training. However, insights such as these about specific situations may not emerge until after the fact.

Organizational Context Questions

Chapter 2 described how S-OJT exists with an organization context. No evaluation of S-OJT can be considered complete until it is determined how the context affected the training. Possibly the most critical issue is the extent of management commitment to the use of S-OJT. S-OJT requires at least as much commitment as off-the-job training approaches, if not more. Commitment means that individuals behave in ways that are consistent with their stated beliefs (Dowling, 1992).

Senior managers often insist that they are committed to the use of S-OJT and then waver when confronted with the realities of such a commitment. For example, it is often necessary to provide replacements for experienced employees who take time off the job to prepare and conduct training. And tools and equipment may have to be purchased for training. Managers should show their commitment by being willing to examine the organization's culture and structure and by determining the changes that have to be made in order to accommodate S-OJT. S-OJT cannot be expected to stand alone. Management commitment is critical to change. Managers must be encouraged to walk their talk on this issue if S-OJT is to be effective.

Another key issue is the way in which S-OJT interacts with other systems in the organization, both positively and negatively. S-OJT interacts with such other organizational systems as:

- production or service-delivery,
- employee development,
- labor–management relations, and
- employee recruitment and selection.

For S-OJT to be effective, it must harmonize with the other systems around it. That is, the goals of one system must be consistent with the goals of the other systems. When supervisors complain that S-OJT is interfering with their ability to get work done, they mean that the goals of the two systems—S-OJT and production—are in conflict.

To summarize, the evaluation questions presented in Figure 10.1 are meant to frame the evaluation of S-OJT. Once the evaluation information has been gathered and conclusions about the results have been drawn, the challenge at hand is to troubleshoot the system.

TROUBLESHOOTING S-OJT

In general, when systems do not achieve their intended goals, we should consider the system components. Examining the information available and deducing the most likely causes enables us to determine the solutions that will be the most effective in correcting the problem. This same approach can be used in troubleshooting S-OJT. That is, when a S-OJT program does not achieve the intended training outputs, we determine why by studying the status of its system components. Troubleshooting S-OJT can occur at two levels of analysis: the training system level and the organization level.

Training System Level

The training system level of analysis focuses on the components of the training system. To determine why one or more of the training outputs was not achieved as expected, each of the training system components should be examined. For S-OJT to achieve the desired outputs, the components must be both adequate and complete.

Training Inputs

In many instances, S-OJT fails to achieve the intended outputs because one of the training inputs is faulty. For example, the trainee and the trainer may be right, but the location selected for the training was not appropriate. Asking the following questions will help determine whether the cause of the problem exists in the training inputs:

1. Is the cause related to the trainee?
   - Did the trainee have the prerequisites?
   - Did the trainee have the personality or temperament suited for this training approach?

2. Is the cause related to the trainer?
   - Did the trainer have appropriate competence in the unit of work?
   - Did the trainer have appropriate competence in being a trainer?

3. Is the cause related to the training location in the job setting?
   - Were the necessary training resources available?
   - Were there scheduling conflicts with ongoing production or service delivery?
   - Was the atmosphere conducive to training and learning?

4. Is the cause related to the unit of work to be learned?
   - Was the task suitable for S-OJT?
   - Was the task analyzed adequately?
   - Was the training module prepared adequately?

Training Process

The training process describes the way in which the S-OJT was carried out. Trainers, often with the best of intentions, sometimes alter the training content or the training delivery in some way, or they deliver the training in different ways to individual trainees. These changes can affect the training outputs in unpredictable ways. Asking the following questions will help determine whether the cause of the problem exists in the training process:

1. Was the trainer ill prepared for his or her presentation(s) of the training material?
2. Was the training content incomplete?
3. Was the delivery of training ineffective or lacking in focus?
4. Was the trainee's performance inadequately tested at the end of training?

Training Outputs

Looking for the cause of problems in training outputs is to question the validity of training goals. This is not as implausible as it may sound. S-OJT closely links training objectives and work expectations. If work expectations change during the design process, training objectives also have to change. If they do not, training is likely to fail. Asking the following questions will help determine whether the cause of the problem exists in the training outputs:

1. Did the work expectations change?
2. Did the trainee's development goals change?
3. Did the requirements of other organizational systems change?

To summarize, problems can be caused by missing or inadequate training system components. The solution depends on the cause of the problem. For example, if the cause is determined to be inconsistency in the delivery of training, one solution is to give trainers a mnemonic device, such as a sticker, that reminds them to use the training events in the order prescribed in the training module. Effective solutions that are simple and low in cost are always preferable. Yet if the S-OJT process is followed, very few remedial solutions should be required.

Organizational Level

Unfortunately, the causes of problems associated with S-OJT are not all located at the training system level. Experience suggests that because causes at the training system level are relatively easy to fix. However, many causes lie at the organization level. Issues that affect S-OJT from the organizational context are far more difficult to fix. Asking the following questions will help determine whether the cause of the problem exists in the organizational context:

1. Does the S-OJT conflict with business issues or priorities that face the organization as a whole?
2. Have the components of a business process been changed in a way to affect the work expectations of people on the process?
3. Does the S-OJT conflict with ongoing change efforts within the organization?
4. Do management, supervisors, or front-line employees place relatively low value on training?
5. Do present agreements between management and unions inhibit S-OJT?
6. Are the goals of training aligned with the goals of related organizational systems?
7. Are the work expectations of experienced employees aligned with the role of being a S-OJT trainer?

8. Are line or staff functions within the organization unwilling to provide the support necessary to manage S-OJT after it has been implemented?

Clearly, the nature of the issues just reviewed makes it unrealistic that managers or HRD professionals acting alone can resolve them in substantive ways. Nevertheless, it can be important to determine which issues are affecting S-OJT, since the resulting information can spur creativity to get around the roadblocks stemming from the organization. For example, managers and union officials have found ways that allows experienced employees to serve as trainers and that maintains the spirit of the original contractual agreement.

Indeed, the troubleshooting of problems whose causes lie in the organizational context usually requires more time and political savvy than the troubleshooting of problems created by training system components. Nevertheless, when the individuals involved understand and value the contributions that S-OJT can make, it is likely that meaningful actions can be taken, even if issues cannot be addressed directly. In many instances, identifying the issues at least gives the parties involved a concrete focus for creative troubleshooting.

CONCLUSION

The last step of the S-OJT process is to evaluate and troubleshoot the training. Evaluation is framed by questions focused on system outputs, processes, and inputs. Evaluation also needs to address the organizational context in which S-OJT occurs. For this reason, troubleshooting should occur at both the training system level and the organization level.

PART THREE
USING STRUCTURED ON-THE-JOB TRAINING

The chapters in Part Two described the steps of the S-OJT process. However, one does not arrive at a successful product simply by performing these steps. Additional issues need to be considered as well. The chapters in Part Three examine the differing contexts in which S-OJT takes place and how to ensure that the training approach is implemented successfully.

Chapter 11
Organizational Change and Structured On-the-Job Training

The global economy has brought about many challenges for organizations, regardless of location. Consider the small manufacturing firms that line the freeway that travels from downtown Taipei to the Chiang Kai-shek International Airport. Many of them display banners outside their buildings proudly announcing that they are ISO 9002 certified. Because of that designation, these companies are presumed to compete on an equal footing with other companies around the world, despite their relatively ramshackle outward appearance. At the same time, these companies share the same challenges of all companies in the global economy. To remain competitive and survive, they must undergo change on a continuous basis.

S-OJT is uniquely suited to facilitate planned organizational change. Consider that most organizational change efforts bring with it changes in the abilities of employees. That is, when organizational change occurs, employees invariably need to be aware of new information, be able to perform their current work better, or be able to perform new work. This chapter covers the following topics:

- Implementation of change through cascade training

- Quality management systems and S-OJT
- Multiskilled employees and employee development

IMPLEMENTATION OF CHANGE THROUGH CASCADE TRAINING

S-OJT can be used to help implement organizational change. That is, regardless of the nature of the change—whether it involves introducing new human resource management software, restructuring the business processes to reduce costs, or producing new products or services altogether to meet a specific market demand—employees must know and do things differently to support the change. Indeed, it has become increasingly clear to many that the success of any organizational change effort comes ultimately from the abilities of the people involved.

The rationale for this statement comes from the literature on the failure of organizational change. The consulting firm A. T. Kearney (1999) notes that managers in 294 European medium-sized companies reported that only one in five organizational change efforts were successful. The remaining efforts made some initial improvements but had failed to sustain them or made no improvements at all. Earlier studies by Goodman and Dean (1983) and Mirvis and Berg (1977) introduced the idea that the persistence of change is a critical issue for organizations to address. Their point was that as much emphasis should be placed on ensuring the acceptance of change as on the change itself.

Thus, organizations face the dual challenges of determining *what* actions to take and *how* to ensure that the actions stay in the organization over the long term. As adapted from Cummings and Worley (2001), Figure 11.1 presents a framework for institutionalizing organizational

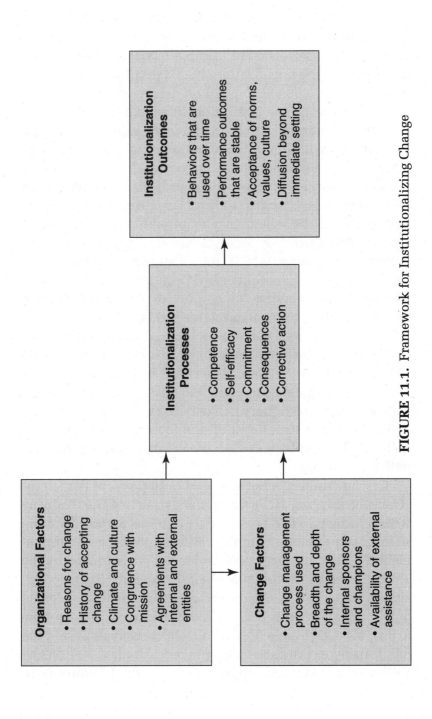

FIGURE 11.1. Framework for Institutionalizing Change

Organizational Factors

- Reasons for change
- History of accepting change
- Climate and culture
- Congruence with mission
- Agreements with internal and external entities

Change Factors

- Change management process used
- Breadth and depth of the change
- Internal sponsors and champions
- Availability of external assistance

Institutionalization Processes

- Competence
- Self-efficacy
- Commitment
- Consequences
- Corrective action

Institutionalization Outcomes

- Behaviors that are used over time
- Performance outcomes that are stable
- Acceptance of norms, values, culture
- Diffusion beyond immediate setting

change (Jacobs, 2002; Jacobs & Russ-Eft, 2001). The framework identifies the factors critical to achieve the institutionalization outcomes, which indicate that change has actually taken hold in the organization. It also proposes that institutionalization outcomes depend on organization factors, intervention factors, and institutionalization processes.

The institutionalization processes are critical since they link directly with institutionalization outcomes, regardless of the change. Foundational to institutionalization processes is whether employees have the appropriate competence to perform what is expected. In turn, employee competence is prerequisite to the self-efficacy required to make the change happen. Self-efficacy is necessary for employees being committed to the change, which in turn allows employees to receive appropriate consequences (Washington, 2001). Finally, with these issues addressed, employees are able to improve the intervention through corrective action.

If employee competence is foundational to organizational change, the question follows how best to provide the required competence. Cascade training is the process of providing the competence necessary to ensure the institutionalization of organizational change (Jacobs, Russ-Eft, & Zidan, 2001). Forms of structured on-the-job training were originally used to implement cascade training, and it continues in that role today.

Cascade training first was used to implement the job instruction training (JIT) programs as part of the Training within Industry (TWI) effort. JIT programs emphasized the training of production employees by supervisors. To implement JIT, plant managers and senior staff were trained by the TWI staff on the benefits of the JIT program. Senior managers trained line managers and supervisors on the benefits of JIT and, along with TWI staff, trained supervisors on how to become a JIT trainer. In the end, supervisors delivered the job training to production employees (Dooley, 1945). The TWI used a systematic approach—from top to bottom—to ensure that all individuals clearly understood their role in making the JIT program successful.

Cascade training was used in the early 1980s by Ford and Xerox to convey general quality concepts throughout the organizations (Galagan, 1990). More recently, numerous organizations have used this approach to disseminate change information through the ranks of employees in a relatively short time.

Four types of cascade training have been proposed: hierarchical, process, role, and project.

Hierarchical

This is perhaps the most common type of cascade training whereby the training follows the vertical structure of the organization, usually starting with upper management and moving downward through the ranks of employees. For instance, Nationwide Insurance used it to implement a new performance appraisal approach throughout the entire organization. The hierarchical approach could also begin from the bottom up, when employees initiate change on their own. The hierarchical approach addresses three issues related to employee competence: (1) which tasks to keep doing, (2) which tasks to stop doing, and (3) which new tasks to begin doing.

Process

The type of cascade training follows the chain of cross-functional relationships of suppliers and customers on a business process. For instance, if a corrective action team at one station of a hard-disk manufacturer improves an operation, the stations both before and after should be informed about the change and its effects on their operations. The process might extend back to suppliers that are external to the organization. The process type ensures that whenever change occurs in one part of a process, other parts become aware of it and respond accordingly.

Role

This type of cascade training follows peer relationships across organizations. For example, managers would train other managers across the organization on aspects of the change effort that impact their role, regardless of functional area. Such an arrangement makes use of the particular insights that only those in that role can provide to explain a new unit of work.

Project

This type of cascade training follows the interconnections of groups, both internal and external, who are working to achieve a goal. One example is when a software package is introduced to a project group, whose members might be located across different locations. The project type ensures that the members and stakeholders understand the change, even though not all members of the project will be affected by it to the same extent.

In sum, organizational change depends on the competence of employees and that cascade training is an effective and efficient means to convey this information across the organization. S-OJT continues to be a primary means to carry out cascade training.

QUALITY MANAGEMENT SYSTEMS AND S-OJT

In the past twenty years or so, many organizations have implemented quality management systems as the focus of the organizational change. Similar to most other major organizational change efforts, quality management systems represent both an opportunity and a challenge. The opportunity is for all employees to be involved in an effort with the promise of increasing job security and improving organizational competitiveness.

At the same time, the challenge is for each person and group in the organization to accept and implement the proposed change, despite the fact that many new practices contradict current practices. Regardless, quality management systems affect both the *amount* of training and the *way* training is conducted in organizations, and in many instances has resulted in using S-OJT.

Quality management systems involve changing a wide range of organizational activities. For instance, the Baldridge National Quality Program (2002) lists seven criteria: leadership, strategic planning, customer and market focus, information and analysis, human resource focus, process management, and business results. Different terms describe quality management systems in organizations, such as *self-managed teams, lean manufacturing, lean enterprise, six sigma,* and *process improvement.* Unfortunately, such names describe only part of the change. In truth, quality management systems call for systemic change.

For instance, *self-managed work teams,* one of several terms commonly used, has been defined as an approach to production or service delivery in which all employees share responsibility and accountability for achieving total customer satisfaction. As Figure 11.2 shows, ten concepts developed by Jones and Jacobs (1990) can be associated with implementing self-managed teams. The concepts are arranged in a wheel since each concept is critical in coordination with the other concepts. Thus, if any one concept, or spoke, is inadequate or is not reconciled with the other concepts, then the quality management system as a whole cannot possibly achieve the intended goals.

The following defines each of the concepts that support self-managed teams:

- *Employee involvement.* The contributions of all employees should occur in a planned way to ensure continuous improvement and quality of work life.

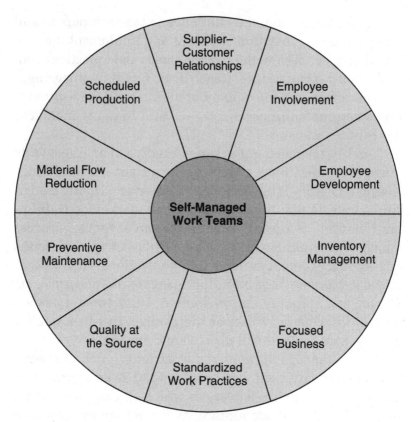

FIGURE 11.2. Components of Self-Managed Work Teams

- *Employee development.* All employees should obtain the training and development experiences required to perform to their fullest potential.
- *Inventory management.* This concept involves maintaining the minimum amount of inventory in the form of raw materials, work-in-process, parts banks, or completed parts or services to deliver to customers on time.
- *Focused business units.* This concept entails grouping related product and service delivery lines so that a particular function becomes responsible and account-

able for all aspects of the products it produces and services it delivers.

- *Standardized work practices.* Explicit work documents should be used to decrease variation in the work.

- *Quality at the source.* All employees should be given the control and resources necessary to meet customer requirements through continuous improvement.

- *Preventive maintenance.* All employees should maintain the equipment, tools, and machinery on a planned basis.

- *Material flow reduction.* Workflows should be organized in a way that reduces excess material and human movement.

- *Scheduled production.* Using pull scheduling, mixed-level scheduling, and quick setups and changes can produce products or deliver services in only the amounts required by the customer.

- *Supplier–customer relationships.* This concept involves establishing long-term relationships with the groups—internally or externally—who supply raw materials and the groups—internally or externally—who receive your parts.

Implementing these aforementioned concepts involves extensive organizational change, which requires addressing new competence requirements. In fact, any one of the concepts has numerous S-OJT topics associated with it. For instance, employee involvement requires appropriate competence to facilitate team meetings, conduct a root-cause analysis, and make presentations to peers—all of which are examples of managerial training. Quality at the source requires appropriate competence to use precision inspection instruments, construct production charts, and adjust equipment based on the results—all of which are examples of technical training. Finally, scheduled production requires appropriate competence to understand pull versus push production systems and maintain scheduling logs—which are examples of awareness training and managerial training respectively.

Perhaps the most commonly known formal quality management system is the International Organization for Standardization (ISO) technical standards. Many organizations—either through their own initiative or through customer requirements—have sought certification as following one of several ISO quality assurance models. The ISO 9000 series, introduced in 1986, presents a set of technical standards that have guided the content of most other quality assurance models. With the introduction of the latest version of the standards in 2000, it remains the dominant global quality management standard.

In addition to the ISO 9000 series of standards (ISO 9001—Fundamentals and Vocabulary; ISO 9001—General Requirements; ISO 9004—Guidance for Performance Improvement; ISO 19011—Guidelines on Quality and Environmental Auditing), an extensive set of quality management standards exist for other purposes. In fact, there are literally dozens of sets of ISO quality management standards, focusing on different business sectors—such as the automotive industry, the extraction of natural resources industry, education and training institutions, and health care providers—and types of organizational activities—such as installation and maintenance of computer software, project management, and equipment testing.

Although each ISO 9000 quality management standard differs in its use, all standards include training. In the ISO 9000 series, Clause 6.2.2—Competence, Awareness and Training under Section 6.2, Human Resources, states:

> The supplier shall determine the necessary competence for personnel performing work affecting quality, provide training or take other actions to satisfy these needs,

evaluate the effectiveness of the actions taken, ensure that its personnel are aware of the relevance and importance of their activities and how they contribute to the achievement of the quality objectives, and maintain appropriate records of education, training, skills, and experience (International Organization for Standardization, 2000).

Perhaps no other single statement affects the amount and nature of training in contemporary organizations. By extension, this standard also affects the usage of S-OJT, particularly in terms of operator training for front-line employees. When ISO audits occur, organizations must show documented evidence of the following activities:

- Assess current and future training requirements.
- Provide the training in a way that addresses the requirements.
- Ensure that only qualified people perform specific units of work.
- Ensure that people understand the importance of their work and its contribution to quality.
- Evaluate the effectiveness of the training provided.
- Maintain records of all personnel training, education, and experiences.

Numerous studies have identified both the positive and negative impacts of ISO on organizations, such as McAdam and McKeown (1999) and Quazi and Padibjo (1998). In terms of its specific effects on training, Quazi and Jacobs (2002) examined the nature and impact of ISO 9001 and ISO 9002 certification on the training and development activities of manufacturing organizations in Singapore. Managers reported on their activities three years before and three years after ISO certification. The results showed significant increases in the HRD processes of needs analysis, training design, training delivery, and training evaluation. The results also indicated a higher number of training dollars spent, more training hours per employee, and a reported improved use of OJT.

The 2002 Baldridge criteria includes the need for training and using appropriate training delivery through Criteria 5.2—Employee Education, Training, Development. However, as a recognition program, the Baldridge criteria have not had the same impact on organizational change as ISO, which is a certification program.

Quality management systems require certain principles to achieve higher quality and lower costs. In turn, these principles emphasize the importance of training and the use of S-OJT in particular. In fact, many organizations, such as Sonoco in its industrial packaging plants, have introduced S-OJT only as part of its quality management efforts.

MULTISKILLED EMPLOYEES AND EMPLOYEE DEVELOPMENT

One of the underlying changes required to implement quality management systems is to increase employee flexibility. For instance, the customer service function of a large nutritional products company sought to have individuals in the contracting, purchasing, and order fulfillment departments be able to perform certain tasks in common, so that when institutional customers called in, their inquiries could be handled more efficiently. Until the change occurred, customer inquiries required numerous phone bounces, unnecessary call-backs, and time delays. Such occurrences were intolerable in a highly competitive environment.

Many organizations seek to increase employee flexibility by developing multiskilled employees. Several employees naturally take on more tasks as part of their jobs. Developing multiskilled employees seeks to prepare individuals to take on expanded tasks. Multiskilled employees are individuals

Production team members work together to perform all operations to produce a completed product. Team members are responsible and accountable for all aspects of the process including safety, quality, and maintenance. Team members conduct and participate in meetings to improve the product, the subassembly process, and the quality of life.

Production Team Members rotate and assist each other in performing the following duties:

A. Operating all equipment in the work area

B. Assembling component parts

C. Ordering production materials and supplies

D. Scheduling production operations

E. Maintaining statistical quality control charts

F. Moving materials and completed subassemblies

G. Troubleshooting safety, quality, and production problems

H. Performing planned maintenance

I. Participating in team meetings

J. Training new team members

K. Preparing production reports

FIGURE 11.3. Job Description and Duties of a Multiskilled Team Member

who can perform a range of work required to produce a completed product or service.

One implication of multiskilled employees is the need to remove narrowly defined job boundaries. For instance, Jones and Jacobs (1990) report how management and union in a manufacturing organization agreed to collapse sixteen job classifications into one classification, the production team member. Figure 11.3 shows the job description and job duties of the new classification. Preliminary results showed that productivity was increased, schedules met with greater ease, and no workers lost their jobs.

To achieve such results, the organization invested heavily in training. In fact, all the cross training on equipment operation was delivered through S-OJT. In addition, S-OJT

delivered the quality, inspection, and troubleshooting training in an off-the-job laboratory. Indeed, several women who
were previously machine operators became expert die set-
ters and later trained others on this important task. Previously, die setting was the exclusive domain of a few men
because of the physical strength it took to lift objects, loosen
and tighten bolts, and so on. However, after several engineering changes increased the reliability and efficiency of
the task, die setting now demanded precision settings rather
than physical abilities.

At least two issues are related to developing multiskilled
employees. First, there is the mistaken belief that the effects
are limited to front-line employees only. In truth, when it is
desirable to have greater employee flexibility, supervisors
and managers undergo dramatic job changes as well and, by
extension, require additional training and development.
Consider that tasks now assigned to multiskilled employees,
such as scheduling, ordering, charting, and training, were
once the responsibility of first-line supervisors. The issue for
supervisors and managers is how to rearrange their duties so
they can be available to facilitate rather than to direct the
work of others. In this instance, supervisors have used a cascade training scheme to train other supervisors on changes
in their jobs.

Second, there are natural limits in developing multiskilled employees. The literature suggests that when individuals become particularly knowledgeable in some area,
their expertise is relatively narrow in scope (Chi et al.,
1988). That is, an individual who can troubleshoot production operations problems cannot necessarily troubleshoot
equipment problems without additional training. Thus, task
carry-over effects seldom occur. In fact, efforts to develop
multiskilled employees often fail because people feel they
cannot assimilate the new information to any depth, all the
while maintaining depth in their current information, which

they wish to protect. Outright resistance occurs when individuals realize that new learning comes at the cost of detrimentally affecting current knowledge and skills.

Greater employee flexibility remains an appropriate organizational goal, and S-OJT is especially appropriate to make that goal occur. However, the following principles must be considered:

- Ensure that the new work is complementary with or logically related to existing work. That is, the work should be similar in nature or have close proximity on the workflows.

- See that individuals understand the inherent intellectual and psychological risks involved in expanding their work expectations.

- Ensure that developing multiskilled employees addresses an actual organizational problem, with shared understanding and involvement about the extent of the problem and the consequences of not taking any action. Multiskilled employees should not be undertaken based on the supposition that a problem exists or a reaction to a management desire.

How to achieve greater employee flexibility through multiskilled employees has become a concern in many organizations. Employee development is the integrated set of planned programs, provided over time, to help ensure that all individuals have the competence necessary to perform to their fullest potential (Jacobs & Washington, 2003). As a process, employee development encompasses the learning of all individuals in organizations—including front-line employees, professionals, or managers—and can be delivered through a range of approaches, including off-the-job and on-the-job training programs, educational programs and seminars, job rotations, self-study materials, and mentoring programs, among others.

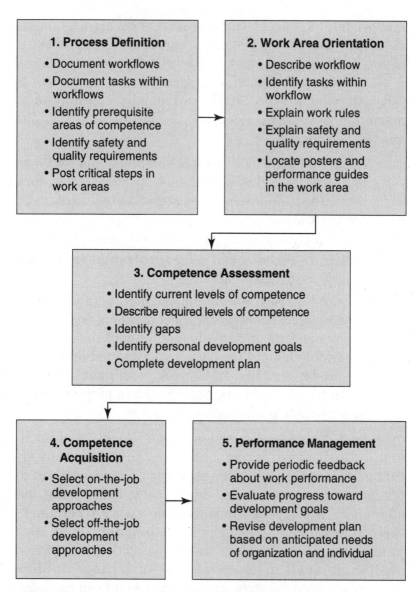

FIGURE 11.4. Front-Line Employee Development System

Figure 11.4 presents an employee development system to identify and meet the needs of front-line employees entering new work areas and their continuing needs over time (Jones & Jacobs, 1994). The system emphasizes the importance of the business process as the organizing principle, not the job per se. The outputs of the system are a development plan to ensure that an employee is prepared to perform in his or her current role and that an employee understands opportunities for advancement and promotion in the organization.

CONCLUSION

S-OJT has played a major role in implementing change in organizations. It is the primary training approach when cascade training informs individuals about change. In addition, S-OJT represents a major way to achieve the training standard when implementing quality management systems. Finally, S-OJT has been used to develop multiskilled employees and as a part of front-line employee development systems.

Chapter 12
Global Perspective of Structured On-the-Job Training

Most perspectives of S-OJT come from a North American tradition of human learning and performance. However, that does not represent all the perspectives. This chapter describes a global perspective of S-OJT.* This information seems important especially since S-OJT places unique demands on trainers and trainees compared to other training approaches. In addition, more and more global organizations use S-OJT, and their use reflects the particular business needs and cultures of their settings. This chapter reviews:

- cross-cultural aspects of S-OJT and
- global uses of S-OJT.

CROSS-CULTURAL ASPECTS OF S-OJT

Recently, an automotive parts supplier in the midwestern United States adopted S-OJT to train new employees on how to sew fabric seat covers, headliners, and other interior

*The author wishes to thank A. Ahad Osman-Gani, professor of international human resource management and development, Nanyang Technological University, Singapore, for his assistance in preparing this chapter.

components. In many respects, the company represents a prime example of the growing management challenges of the global economy. Located close to its U.S. customers, the company is part of a larger auto parts supply company based in Japan. As a result, most senior managers are Japanese nationals who come to work on temporary assignment. Supervisors in the organization tend to be U.S. citizens, and the front-line employees have been counted to come from fourteen different nations—from Russia to Laos to Ethiopia. Although individuals in the company represent a wide mixture of races, religions, and languages, they share the mission of making quality interior automotive components for its customer.

As S-OJT has been used in this organization, managers have asked the following questions: Are the apparent cultural differences among employees meaningful in terms of the training effectiveness? That is, will training outcomes differ just because a female supervisor who comes from Ohio trains a front-line female employee who comes from Ethiopia? Will training outcomes differ just because a Japanese manager trains the supervisors?

Part of the answer comes from the literature on national culture and its influence on organizational behavior, and part comes from understanding the unique demands of S-OJT on trainers and trainees.

National Culture and Training Effectiveness

From the cross-cultural literature, national culture affects a wide range of organizational functioning, such as how people make decisions, accept new technology, and take on management approaches (Osman-Gani, 2000). In fact, research has shown that national culture can be as strong a determinant of individual behavior as is organizational culture (Osman-Gani & Jacobs, 1996; Hofstede, 2001). Culture describes the characteristic behaviors that identify a group of people, based on a range of shared determinants, such as ethnicity, language, and religion.

Cross-cultural researchers often use national boundaries as proxies for identifying cultures, since the political entity yields another layer of experience to shape behavior. For instance, some observers say that the ethnic Chinese who live in Singapore differ, if only in subtle ways, from the ethnic Chinese who live in Malaysia or in China, just because of their differing national experiences in the last forty years.

The global economy has complicated the effects of national culture because of the greater degree of interaction and contact among various peoples. More and more, people now move toward the demand for their competence, regardless of location. For example, many computer engineers from the Indian subcontinent now work in Ireland. Many production workers in the Netherlands come from Turkey and Morocco. Many service representatives in Kuwaiti hotels come from the Philippines. As part of their expatriate assignment with electronics manufacturers, numerous Korean managers now live in Eastern European countries. More than two million North Americans now work for foreign employers (Chaney & Martin, 2000). As a result, there is a greater chance today that when individuals interact in organizations, they represent a mismatch of national cultures.

Questions remain about the specific relationship between national cultural and training effectiveness (Osman-Gani, 2000). That is, deriving useful principles from research and practice is not altogether possible. Some unresolved questions include the following:

- Should we strive to match national cultures during training?
- How should we address mismatches in national cultures during training?
- When planning a training program, should individuals from highly collectivist cultures, such as some countries

in Africa or Asia, receive training approaches emphasizing group learning?

- Should individuals from highly sequential cultures, such as Anglo-Saxon countries, receive training approaches emphasizing competition and individual achievement?

Considering these questions raises the following issue. On the one hand, sound human resource development practice emphasizes the need to address trainee characteristics as part of the training design process. On the other hand, an equally valid principle holds that each person is an individual in his or her own right, and people should not be given certain training approaches, just because of the presumed cultural influences on their preferences.

While specific information about national culture and training effectiveness is not available, learning preferences are a fundamental part of national culture and, thus, become a potentially important variable to mediate training effectiveness.

Unique Demands of S-OJT

Whatever relationship exists between national culture and training effectiveness seems even more pronounced with S-OJT. In general, trainers and trainees undergo relatively more anxiety when using S-OJT than most other training approaches, simply because S-OJT requires an intense level of contact between them. In contrast, consider a typical training classroom that, in spite of the trainer's best efforts otherwise, does not involve all trainees to the same extent. In fact, in a classroom setting, the burden of the instructional effort lies mostly with the trainer, who is doing the performing, while trainees can remain passive for much of the session.

In contrast, the instructional burden in S-OJT is shared between the trainer and trainee. Indeed, S-OJT represents a heightened sense of awareness on the part of both the trainer and the trainee. When following the training events, the trainer must deliver the training effectively to ensure that the trainee can respond effectively. In turn, the trainee must attend to the trainer's presentation so that he or she is ready to respond when requested by the trainer. Whatever cultural differences exist between trainer and trainee are more likely exposed in this intense environment.

While the intensity of S-OJT is often desirable, the setting might not necessarily match the cultural preferences of the individuals involved. For instance, the Confucian culture has influenced individual and organizational cultures in many Asian countries (Hofstede, 1996) and likely influences the use of S-OJT as well. Trainees in Taiwan, Korea, and Singapore have been observed to be especially hesitant to ask questions during the training, even when queried repeatedly by the trainer. Since the trainer is a person of authority, asking questions might show disrespect for the trainer and the trainer's ability to instruct. As such, many trainees remain silent during the training session and prefer to resolve questions on their own, which could have undesirable effects.

In addition, trainees in these same countries become unusually anxious when they are asked to respond following the presentation of the content. Trainees want to avoid appearing vulnerable or inept in front of the trainer. All of these behaviors could have Confucian cultural influences. Another perspective is that the intimate setting of S-OJT allows trainees to save face—an important aspect in many Asian cultures—when trainees make errors during the learning process. The learning occurs within a more protected social setting.

Given that national culture influences training effectiveness to some extent and the unique demands of S-OJT, it seems prudent to consider the following suggestions when implementing this training approach:

- Identify the individuals who will be involved in the training—the trainers and trainees—and determine whether they come from the same or different national or personal cultural backgrounds, such as language and ethnicity.

- Surmise whether the culture will likely affect training effectiveness. For instance, if there is a mismatch in language or ethnicity, determine whether these variables might inhibit understanding of the content. Or if there is a match in these variables, determine whether the training is best suited to their shared preferences. Be aware that cultural differences need not always affect training effectiveness. And cultural similarities need not always guarantee success.

- Make the individuals involved in the training aware of any cultural differences and alert them of possible issues that might arise because of the differences.

- Observe the training interactions to determine whether culture in fact plays a role in training effectiveness.

- Ask trainees and trainers at the conclusion of the training whether they were aware of any special difficulties, such as the trainer's way of addressing the trainee, the trainer's customary behavior during the training, and the trainer's perception of the trainee's willingness to respond when requested.

- Use the insights and information gathered during this process to guide the design and delivery of future training sessions.

GLOBAL USES OF S-OJT

A growing number of case studies report the use of S-OJT in global organizations. The following case studies are instructive because they at once show that the use of S-OJT is affected by differing national cultures and that global organizations are affected by similar challenges.

Sullivan, Brechin, and Lacoste (1998) describe a case study on how structured on-the-job training was used to train health care providers in Zimbabwe and Kenya on IUD insertion techniques. The training provided clinical skills to field service providers and covered the same content as an existing instructor-led course. The researchers report numerous benefits in terms of provider performance and delivery of quality services and expressed the goal of expanding the use of structured on-the-job training into other health care areas.

In Germany, most structured on-the-job training occurs within the apprenticeship system for new workers. Most apprenticeships are run by companies, overseen by unions and employer organizations. Within the apprenticeship model, Dehnbostel (2001) describes the concept of training islands used in many large German manufacturing companies. Training islands are areas near where production occurs and is dedicated to developing skilled production employees through structured on-the-job training. Training islands have the same layout and resources of the nearby production area, but they are reserved strictly for training purposes.

Lee and Yun (2002) report how the six sigma quality management model was used to implement structured on-the-job training at LG Electronics in South Korea. The authors report how engineers' performance on a specific task was improved beyond the expected goal through the use of structured on-the-job training.

Al-Muzaini, Al-Keane, and Al-Awadi (2002) note that structured on-the-job training is the primary development approach used for new-hire refinery engineers with the Kuwait National Petroleum Company. The authors report dramatic reductions in development time and improved learning outcomes of engineers.

Stolovitch and Ngoa-Nguele (2002) describe how structured on-the-job training was used in a brewery setting in Cameroon, making the point that this training approach is especially suited for use in developing nations because it does not require expensive technology to deliver and makes effective use of the available know-how.

In Japan, structured on-the-job training is the primary means of training employees and is used mostly in the context of organizations using the "Shokuno Shikaku Seido," or job classification competency matrix (Yutaka, 1999). Indeed, most Japanese firms, regardless of size, offer little if any off-the-job training programs. Every supervisor and manager is responsible for carrying out structured on-the-job training. In this approach, the training is used over a long-term period as part of career ladders to deepen and broaden skills and to facilitate greater flexibility in taking on job assignments within a work team (Brown & Reich, 2002). Using structured on-the-job training to support career ladders is based on relatively long employee employment, an assumption that has been challenged in recent economic times.

Finally, several unreported structured on-the-job training case studies have been developed in Taiwan, some through the China Productivity Center (CPC), a government-linked organization that provides consulting services to address organizational change, information technology, and human capital issues. Many of the case studies describe how employees in clean-room situations have been trained among semiconductor manufacturing firms, such as Taiwan Semiconductor Manufacturing Company, located in the Hshinchu Science-Based Industrial Park.

Perhaps other than the United States, no two countries have shown greater interest in structured on-the-job training than the Netherlands and Singapore. Although their interest stems from different sources, each country deserves special focus here.

The Netherlands

Interest in on-the-job training and learning in the Netherlands has been driven mostly by a groundswell of activity among its HRD practitioner and academic communities. Faculty groups at several of its major universities, including those at Utrecht University and Twente University, have focused almost their entire scholarly attention on these and related topics.

Individual researchers, such as Jan de Jong at Utrecht University, have been instrumental in bringing Dutch research and practice into the broader human resource development scholarly literature. For instance, de Jong (1993) and de Jong and Bogaards (2002) describe in some depth the intentions, actualities, and results of how structured on-the-job training was used for production employees in a Dutch company that makes cans and battery cases. Indeed, the attention to S-OJT and related workplace learning topics by researchers in this country has become recognized internationally.

Reasons for the interest in structured on-the-job training are said to come from at least two sources. First, as a relatively small trading nation, the Netherlands has traditionally searched for the best practices in all areas of endeavor to maximize its influence. In this sense, some Dutch researchers report being initially attracted to this training approach because of the reported successes achieved in the TWI project during World War II. Subsequent interest comes from the practical need to help ensure the competitiveness Dutch companies.

Second, the Netherlands has historically been influenced by the German tradition of apprenticeships and working with *meisters* in the work setting, although this training system never developed to the same extent in the Netherlands. In any case, from this cultural exposure, training and learning on the job continues as an enduring topic of interest among managers and researchers alike.

Today, the Netherlands has become a point of reference on structured on-the-job training among the members of the European Community. Eight major research projects, funded through the Leonardo da Vinci program, were conducted by Dutch researchers from 1995 to 1999. These projects follow the Dutch tradition of connecting useful research with management practices.

De Gram and Glaude (2000) report on the various structured on-the-job training research projects funded by the Leonardo da Vinci program. The report reviews structured on-the-job training research conducted in the Netherlands, structured on-the-job training practices in the Netherlands, and case studies from Dutch companies. The report represents the high level of interest in on-the-job training and learning among HRD researchers and practitioners in the Netherlands.

Singapore

Interest in structured on-the-job training in Singapore has primarily come from programs instituted through its various government-linked organizations. In contrast to the Netherlands, HRD researchers and practitioners have followed the lead first taken by these government initiatives. Since the 1990s, the National Productivity and Standards Board—now known as the Standards, Productivity, and Innovation for Growth (SPRING)—collaborated with Seiko Instruments in Japan to develop OJT modules to show companies how to develop and implement structured on-the-job training. In 1993, the OJT 2000 Plan was formally launched with the goal of institutionalizing structured on-the-job training in organizations and to train 100,000 workers by 2000 (Pious, 1994).

The OJT 2000 initiative included a range of resources for organizations, including seminars for managers, courses for OJT trainers, generic OJT course modules, a computer-based management system for tracking employee progress, and financial support to companies seeking to implement structured on-the-job training. The National Productivity and Standards Board functioned more as a resource linker for companies. In addition, the Institute for Technical Education (ITE), the postsecondary training schools in Singapore, contributed by offering the Certified On-the-Job Training Certificate to recognize companies using structured on-the-job training appropriately.

Numerous case studies have been reported through internal SPRING documents describing the experiences of companies using structured on-the-job training, including high-tech manufacturing, retail, and service companies. For instance, Otis Elevator Company, designated as a SPRING model company, reported how it provided structured on-the-job training to escalator service technicians. The results showed a substantial decrease in training time for new technicians and reduced rework. In addition, the public media have also been enlisted to announce new plans and promote the use of structured on-the-job training (see, e.g., Osman, 2000).

Subsequent to the OJT 2000 Plan, SPRING introduced the OJT 21 Plan in 2000 with the goal to train 500,000 workers by 2005. Part of the emphasis of the OJT 21 Plan was on assisting small- and medium-sized companies, which form the backbone of the Singapore economy. It is not surprising that Jacobs and Osman-Gani (1999) found that structured on-the-job training is the most frequently used training approach in Singapore organizations, across all business sectors.

Two additional initiatives from SPRING have provided further context to the OJT 21 Plan. The first initiative is the

People Developer certificate, which recognizes organizations that have systematically reviewed their human resource practices, adopted a structured approach to staff development, improved the effectiveness of training, and as a result shown better business results. Similar to an ISO 9000 audit, companies must undergo a review to receive the certification, which allows them to display the logo on official company publications.

The second initiative is the CREST program (Critical Enabling Skills Training), a certificate program for individuals, which focuses on how to attain seven competencies that respond to the changing job requirements of the knowledge-based economy. Of interest here is the first CREST competency, Learning-to-Learn.

Up to 80 percent of the costs of these various programs can be paid for through the Skills Development Fund, supported by a levy placed on employers and contributions from employees. Perhaps no other country compares to Singapore in its determination on the part of government planners to ensure that employees can respond to global market demands. In this context, structured on-the-job training seems an obvious focus of their attention.

CONCLUSION

Structured on-the-job training has become a global phenomenon, primarily because organizations are subject to the same economic challenges regardless of their location. National culture influences many aspects of organizational functioning and presumably affects training effectiveness as well. Consideration needs to be taken when trainers and trainees differ in their national cultures. As a global phenomenon, structured on-the-job training has been used in a wide range of global settings. The developments in the Netherlands and Singapore have been highlighted here since these countries have demonstrated a particular interest in this training approach.

Chapter 13
Workforce Development and Structured On-the-Job Training

Until recently, S-OJT has been mostly used to train individuals already employed in organizations. That is, a specific business issue was identified, and then S-OJT was used to address the issue. While S-OJT continues to be used in this way, an emerging trend is to use it to address societal goals within the context of workforce development. The importance of using S-OJT to address workforce development goals cannot be underestimated. Indeed, using S-OJT in this way will largely define the nature of this training approach in the coming years.

This chapter discusses S-OJT in relation to the following topics:

- Workforce development
- Economic development and productivity centers
- The Workforce Investment Act
- School-to-work initiatives for youth
- Apprenticeships

WORKFORCE DEVELOPMENT

The preceding chapters have discussed the proven training efficiency and training effectiveness of S-OJT. This conclusion is based on the case studies that report how it helped achieve important organizational outcomes. The efficiency and effectiveness of S-OJT have also come to the attention of those who seek to achieve societal outcomes within the context of workforce development. Workforce development has broader goals than to improve organizational performance, though that goal certainly falls within its scope of the interest.

Among the challenges of the global economy is the need for societies to prepare individuals more systematically to enter careers, to upgrade their knowledge and skills continuously, and to retrain them for new careers when necessary. No one organization can address these challenges alone. Instead, these challenges require the cooperation of both public and private resources.

Workforce development is the process of coordinating school, agency, and organization-based training and education programs such that they provide the opportunity for individuals to realize a sustainable livelihood and organizations to compete better in the global marketplace (Jacobs & Hawley, 2002). Workforce development programs focus on four societal issues:

1. How schools and agencies prepare individuals to enter or reenter the workforce

2. How organizations provide learning opportunities to improve workforce performance

3. How organizations respond to changes that affect workforce effectiveness

4. How individuals undergo life transitions related to workforce participation (Jacobs, 1999)

Structured on-the-job training has received attention by workforce development professionals in the context of helping address these issues.

ECONOMIC DEVELOPMENT AND PRODUCTIVITY CENTERS

In one form or another, local and national governments throughout the world have established economic development and productivity centers. These centers provide resource assistance to help businesses and industries grow and cope with change. Some national productivity centers are the result of post–World War II reconstruction efforts, while other centers have been established more recently. Several of these centers explicitly offer S-OJT as a service to their client organizations.

For instance, the EnterpriseOhio Network serves as a point of collaboration among Ohio's community and technical colleges and university regional campuses in delivering training, education, and consulting services. Network representatives link companies in need with appropriate resources to address competitiveness issues. Smith, Just, and Prigelmeier (2002) report how they implemented structured on-the-job training in two Ohio companies, using resources provided through the EnterpriseOhio Network. The emphasis of the case studies is on the process used to analyze the tasks.

Also, EnterpriseOhio Network (2002) reports a project in which structured on-the-job training was used to cross-train employees in a warehouse distribution center. The report states that employees achieved the targeted productivity levels four to five times faster than the unstructured OJT approach previously used.

The Center for Entrepreneurial Studies and Development (CESD) is a nonprofit organization affiliated with West

Virginia University to support that state's economy through its workforce and the organizations that employ the workers. Molnar, Watts, and Byrd (1998) report that structured on-the-job training is used by CESD to address business issues for a range of employees. They also state that structured on-the-job training documents the experiences of senior employees so that their practices can become part of the entire organization.

Many of these programs are funded through local grants or through federal funds provided through the 1974 Trade Adjustment Assistance program, the 1993 North American Free Trade Agreement Transitional Adjustment Assistance program, or the 1993 Trade Readjustment Allowance. These programs assist workers who lose their jobs because of increased imports or shifts in production to Mexico or Canada.

Chapter 12 discussed the Productivity, Standards and Innovation Board in Singapore and the China Productivity Center in Taiwan, as both promoting the use of S-OJT. In addition, the Korean Productivity Center encourages the use of S-OJT through its programs for small and medium-sized companies.

WORKFORCE INVESTMENT ACT

Structured on-the-job training also figures prominently in the delivery of services related to the Workforce Investment Act (WIA) of 1998. The legislation fostered the consolidation of the many federal employment and training programs and services, requiring states to use a centralized service delivery structure—or the one-stop system. The system is intended to be customer focused to help individuals access the tools they need to manage their careers. The system is also intended to help companies find the skilled workers they need to compete and succeed in business. In practice, WIA programs are administered through local governments and advisory boards.

WIA programs help individuals by increasing their employment and earnings potential, improving their educational and occupational skills, and, in some cases, reducing their dependency on welfare. Workforce investment activities authorized by WIA are provided to serve two primary customer groups: job seekers, including dislocated workers, youth, incumbent workers; and new entrants to the workforce and employers, looking for employees. In general, for individuals, WIA provides temporary assistance for families, apprenticeship opportunities, employment matches, and training and education information. For employers, it provides resources for placing job orders and obtaining referrals, labor market data, information and referrals on training resources, and business assistance.

Among the WIA programs of highest appeal is the OJT program. In this scheme, local employers are identified that will take on trainees to learn specific skills over a period of time. OJT candidates are prescreened and approved by the organization. When a match is made, an OJT contract is drawn up with the employer, including how much the organization will be reimbursed for the wages paid to the trainee. The benefit to individuals is that they can learn and earn at the same time, along with the potential for being hired by the employer at the end of the OJT. For employers, they have an added employee, without shouldering the entire cost burden. At the end, employers have trained individuals whom they might be able to hire.

To suggest that the OJT delivered by employers is structured or planned to any extent would be incorrect. In fact, little information is available about the OJT experience, and most employers are small- or medium-sized organizations, with limited training resources for their own regular employees. However, as demands increase for greater program accountability, the nature of the OJT experience will likely come under greater scrutiny.

SCHOOL-TO-WORK INITIATIVES

In 1994, the School-to-Work Opportunities Act was enacted to provide support for local partnerships between businesses, employer organizations, unions, and education to prepare youth for high-skill careers. While school-to-work programs differ across localities, they must contain three basic components: (1) school-based learning based on academic and business-defined standards; (2) work-based learning composed of career exploration, work experience, training, and mentoring in organizations; and (3) connecting activities that integrate classroom experiences with the work-based learning.

Hoerner and Wehrley (2000) emphasize work-based learning as a critical outcome of school-to-work programs and promote OJT as one strategy to achieve this goal. Cooperating employers are identified that will take on the students, at times with a financial inducement. The students work and learn in the organization for a part of their school term along with their academic studies.

Use of OJT with school-to-work programs raises at least two issues. First, OJT emphasizes the acquisition of specific skills, which might not be the same aim of the school-to-work program. Because they focus on secondary-level youth, school-to-work programs more likely emphasize career exploration through mentoring and job shadowing rather than specific work skills through OJT. Thus, OJT is likely to fill a niche in a school-to-work experience.

Second, given the appropriateness of OJT in a school-to-work situation, questions remain about the quality of the OJT experience. Similar to employers involved in WIA programs, few employers involved in school-to-work programs are likely to use structured on-the-job training. Again, most of these organizations are small- to medium-sized companies with limited resources.

However, in spite of these issues, OJT remains an important aspect of school-to-work programs. OJT can be especially useful for students who struggle with academics and require hands-on experiences to understand the relevance of the information.

APPRENTICESHIPS

Apprenticeships have emerged as another form of training to achieve workforce development goals. Apprenticeships focus on preparing individuals for occupations by combining on-the-job training with related theoretical and practical classroom experiences. After a period of some disinterest, apprenticeships have received renewed interest primarily as part of WIA and school-to-work programs. For instance, Arizona lists more than 120 apprenticeship programs across a range of occupations, with more than 3,000 individuals enrolled in apprenticeship programs. In Maryland, 207 occupations are listed, with over 17,000 apprentice graduates. Depending on the occupation, apprenticeship programs are operated and sponsored by employers, employer associations, or joint union–management boards. Government bodies usually oversee and register apprenticeship programs based on guidelines from the Department of Labor, Bureau of Apprenticeship Training. Apprentices are paid through the sponsoring agency.

Until recently, most apprenticeships have been time based in nature, requiring that a specific period of time be spent between the trainer and the apprentice. However, more and more apprenticeships have become competency based, meaning that the apprentices can complete the training when they can adequately perform the identified component

tasks, however long that might take. As such, apprenticeships have become much more similar in form to structured
on-the-job training.

In fact, in describing their apprenticeship programs,
structured on-the-job training has been mentioned as being a
critical component of the experience. For instance, several
states—such as Maryland, New Hampshire, Alaska, and
South Dakota, among others—specifically use structured on-
the-job training to describe the work component of the apprenticeship. In addition, the Enterprise and Career Education Foundation in Australia, a national organization that
helps youth make good career choices, has developed over
260 apprenticeship programs that combine classroom learning with structured on-the-job training. Finally, the New Or-
leans Electrical Joint Apprenticeship & Training Committee
states that its electrical construction apprenticeships combine supervised structured on-the-job training with related
theoretical instruction.

Integrating structured on-the-job training with apprenticeships seems like a natural and productive relationship.
In general, apprenticeships have a long tradition of helping
individuals enter skilled and technical occupations. However, two inherent needs have always seemed to surround
the apprenticeship experience, which structured on-the-job
training could help address. The first need has been to identify in explicit terms what is supposed to be learned during
the apprenticeship. That is, what are the major duties, tasks,
and task components of the occupation? The development
of S-OJT modules based on the specific units of work could
easily address this need.

The second need has been to ensure that trainers have
the ability to impart the training effectively. Unfortunately,
as discussed in Chapter 6, many OJT trainers use the same
training techniques that were used in their own training, regardless of whether they liked it or not. S-OJT could help

develop trainers in ways that could increase the effectiveness and the efficiency of the apprenticeship experience.

CONCLUSION

This chapter has reported how structured on-the-job training is used to achieve workforce development goals. In truth, the amount of structured on-the-job training programs that are part of WIA programs, school-to-work initiatives, and apprenticeship programs remains uncertain. In fact, the OJT being used in most instances may actually be unstructured in nature. Nevertheless, these programs have profoundly increased the amount of OJT being conducted in organizations and have widened the range of trainees receiving OJT. It seems only a matter of time before these OJT programs will undergo greater scrutiny and receive greater attention to their planning and implementation. For this reason, these various workforce development programs will likely influence to a great extent the future nature of S-OJT.

Chapter 14

Change Management Process and Issues in Using Structured On-the-Job Training

The individual steps of the S-OJT process are only part of successfully implementing S-OJT. Managing the change process is equally important. This chapter addresses these topics:

- Defining the change management process for S-OJT
- Issues of concern in using S-OJT

CHANGE MANAGEMENT PROCESS

The reader should not believe that using the S-OJT process was all that it took to produce a successful training program. While the process shows how to design, deliver, and evaluate S-OJT, it does not guarantee that the organization, regardless of the business need and context, will automatically accept the training approach. To be most successful, S-OJT should be viewed from a change management perspective. This perspective states that both the organization and S-OJT are systems and that the two systems have to be reconciled if they are to achieve mutually dependent goals. Without this

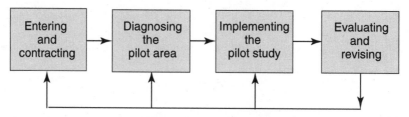

FIGURE 14.1. S-OJT Change Management Process

perspective, S-OJT is likely to be short-lived (Jacobs & Russ-Eft, 2001).

Figure 14.1, based on a model of organization development by Cummings and Worley (2001), shows the change management process for S-OJT. The process essentially treats the S-OJT as a pilot project having a starting point and ending point and a goal of institutionalizing the use of S-OJT in the long term. The change management process seems appropriate for use regardless of whether the S-OJT is introduced by an internal employee, most likely the HRD manager on behalf of senior management, or an external consultant. Either party can be considered part of the team, responsible for facilitating the improvement process in the organization. The change management process has four steps: entering and contracting, diagnosing the pilot area, implementing the pilot study, and evaluating and revising. The remainder of this section examines these four steps.

Entering and Contracting

The first stage of the change management process has two stages: entering into negotiation and developing the contract with the client.

Entering

The entering stage is intended to determine the fit between S-OJT and the organization and whether the organization is prepared to commit the necessary resources to ensure success. Chapters 2 and 10 suggest that S-OJT systems are affected by issues arising in the organizational context. The entering stage helps identify the issues that have the most importance and predict their likely effects on a S-OJT program. Management can then decide whether to proceed.

The entering stage usually involves meeting with senior managers from a number of different areas, including production, human resources, safety, and engineering, to discuss the problems and opportunities that confront the organization. These meetings are critical, since they provide a sense of the organization's readiness for change. Some have referred to these activities as courtship, since each party is looking at the other as a potential partner, and no commitment is made until both parties have gathered adequate information to move forward.

The following questions summarize key indicators that can determine whether S-OJT fits an organization:

- Is senior management willing to commit resources to support S-OJT?

- Are managers and supervisors willing to host a S-OJT pilot project in their work area?

- Are off-site training programs already present in the organization? Are they valued?

- In what ways could S-OJT address the organization's most pressing needs?

- What priorities do senior executives express for human resources?

- Have contractual agreements between union and management been altered to reflect a desire to use S-OJT?

- Have internal planning committees been established to review the feasibility of using S-OJT and to address any issues that may inhibit its use?

- Have line and staff managers called for changes in the mission and policies of the human resource development function?

- What kind of ongoing change efforts, such as safety awareness or continuous quality improvement programs, are already in place? Can S-OJT play a role in the existing programs?

- Is the human resource development function capable of implementing the S-OJT, and are other logical functional areas willing to manage the S-OJT program?

The feasibility of proceeding with the project can be determined from the answers to these questions.

It is reasonable to expect that S-OJT will not be appropriate in some organizations. In fact, information that emerged during the entering stage has led us to walk away from more than one organization that was interested in using S-OJT but that was deficient in some aspect that would have made the success of a S-OJT project unlikely. The specific issues that can hinder the project should be clearly identified for the client.

Contracting

If S-OJT seems feasible for the organization, the second stage is to develop a contract specifying the particulars of the project. Developing a contract is often an iterative process whereby the contract is revised repeatedly to ensure that the language suits all parties. Even if the specific location has not been selected for the pilot study, it is often possible for the contract to specify the broad functional areas, such as customer service operations, retail sales, production, or maintenance, which will host the S-OJT project.

The contract should spell out the following items:

- Goals of the project
- Deliverables of the project

- Probable pilot study areas
- Roles of the individuals inside and outside the organization
- Financial, physical, and human resources that the organization will provide in support of the project
- Evaluation criteria
- Total costs
- Time line
- Renegotiation statement

Figure 14.2 shows a portion of a contract for an organization intending to implement S-OJT. This contract was generated by an external consultant, but it would be equally useful for internal HRD staff.

Diagnosing the Pilot Area

The next step of the change management process is to conduct a detailed study of the problems or issues that affect specific functional areas with the organization and to select a specific location for the pilot study.

In general, an in-depth analysis of the organizational situation requires problems within functional areas to be documented in terms of gaps between the current levels of performance and the desired levels of performance. Unfortunately, managers are often not able to provide group or individual performance information in this way. As stated, S-OJT should be used only when a documented performance problem caused by a lack of appropriate levels of competence has been determined to be the cause of the problem. For this reason, the diagnosis stage may have to include a performance analysis. If it does, the contract agreement may have to be renegotiated. Having performance information framed in terms of current levels of performance and desired levels of performance is especially critical for the success of the project.

Our understanding is that your organization is now required to certify its technicians to perform certain tasks critical for service delivery. In addition, S-OJT has been selected as the most appropriate training approach to ensure that these employees learn the information in the most effective and efficient means possible.

Proposed Goals

Based on the above understanding, we propose to achieve the following project goals:

A.   Provide an overview to management about S-OJT.

B.   Identify tasks appropriate for S-OJT based on a range of criteria, including a financial forecasting analysis.

C.   Train experienced technicians and supervisors to deliver S-OJT.

D.   Assist technical training staff to develop training modules.

E.   Prepare a plan to evaluate the S-OJT.

Deliverables

The deliverables of the proposed project are the following:

A.   One-day presentation to senior managers and supervisors on S-OJT. The presentation will be designed to (1) inform them about S-OJT; (2) discuss the potential benefits of this training approach, based on our experiences in other organizations; (3) demonstrate how S-OJT is actually carried out, including example documents from other organizations; and (4) respond to questions and issues about the use of S-OJT.

B.   Provide a short report that presents the financial forecasting analysis based on the information provided to the consultants. This information will be presented as part of the one-day presentation.

C.   Two-day session with the technical training staff on developing training documents to be used with S-OJT

D.   One-day training session with experienced employees on delivering S-OJT

E.   A plan that describes the evaluation questions to be asked, focusing on the training process and training outcomes, the sources of information, and the data-gathering methods

F.   Written final report and management presentation along with line personnel and supervisors reporting the results of the evaluation

FIGURE 14.2. S-OJT Contract Components

Documenting the performance problems is likely to reveal one or more potential locations for the pilot study. A pilot study resembles full-scale implementation, but it is limited to specific areas. The following criteria are used to select the locations for S-OJT pilot studies:

- The interest of area managers and supervisors in hosting a pilot study and their readiness to do so
- The interest of front-line employees in those areas in participating in the pilot project
- The representativeness of the work being done in those areas
- The consequences of the problems as documented by performance analysis in those areas
- The overall chance of success in implementing S-OJT in those areas

As part of the diagnosis step, key individuals may be asked to provide an overview of S-OJT to managers, supervisors, union leaders, and other key stakeholders within the potential pilot study locations. The management overviews usually follow this order:

1. Discuss organizational issues and ways of addressing the issues
2. Discuss how employee competence is affected by the issues.
3. Discuss how S-OJT can address competence needs.
4. Provide examples of S-OJT and unstructured OJT.
5. Describe the forecasted financial and nonfinancial benefits of S-OJT.
6. Describe the general steps of an action plan.
7. Allow for further discussion.

Even if the client has not requested such a session, it is important to provide the management overview. Experience shows that it helps participants begin to envision what S-OJT would look like in their areas, and it gives us an opportunity to share the experiences—both positive and negative of other organizations.

Implementing the Pilot Study

Once the location for the pilot study has been selected, the action plan can be carried out. The steps of the action plan specify the sequence of events that will take place to implement S-OJT. As a rule, these steps combine the basic steps for developing S-OJT as presented in this book with information that accommodates the needs of the organization.

For example, it is sometimes necessary to give various parts of the process different names to make the action plan consistent with the vocabulary used in the organization. It may also be necessary to give the steps a new sequence. For example, you may have to select and train the S-OJT trainers before you perform any of the other steps of the S-OJT process. Finally, steps sometimes have to be added to the action plan to meet the expectations of the contract. These additional steps can include:

- conducting a performance analysis,
- preparing the case studies at the conclusion of the pilot study, and
- presenting the case studies to management.

To summarize, this stage of the change management process combines the process presented in this book with information obtained from the organization.

Evaluating and Revising

The last step of the change management process has two stages: evaluating the pilot project and making any necessary revisions.

Evaluating

As stated in Chapter 10, the primary purpose of evaluating S-OJT is for improvement. The evaluation is not meant to support a summative judgment on whether to keep S-OJT in place unless unforeseen events have made its continuance impossible.

Case studies are the primary means of communicating the results of the evaluation. Each case study presents the information related to the design, implementation, and evaluation of S-OJT in a specific pilot study location. Case studies should be prepared by those participating in the pilot study location. A collaborative process helps ensure that the information presented is accurate, objective, and fair.

The case studies can be presented to stakeholders in a final written report or an oral presentation. Employees who helped prepare the case studies should be listed as coauthors.

Case studies have proved to have a powerful effect on management decisions regarding S-OJT. They are not fabricated events; they tell the actual stories of real people within the organization.

Revising

If the case study approach is used properly, it can be extremely useful in identifying areas for revision. In most organizations, several pilot study locations can operate concurrently. When several case studies are available, they can be viewed more easily if presented in a matrix. The names of the locations are placed across the top of the matrix. The left side of the matrix lists the evaluation questions as described in Chapter 10. The evaluation data gathered from each pilot location completes the individual cells. The resulting display analyzes and synthesizes the entire pilot study effort. Each column in the matrix shows the evaluation results from one pilot study location, and each row compares the answers of individual locations to a single evaluation question. Distinct patterns and insights for revision can emerge when the matrix is viewed from two perspectives.

ISSUES OF CONCERN

Throughout this book, S-OJT has been shown to enhance the performance of organizations in important ways. At this point, some issues need to be identified that can diminish its effectiveness if they are not addressed. In this section, seven such issues are discussed: undue time burden, unwillingness to train, trainer's work expectations, employee development, other forms of training in the work setting, use of the deductive method, and the role of HRD staff.

Undue Time Burden

One issue that managers often express is that S-OJT places an undue time burden on employees who have already been asked to do more on the job. This opinion has been expressed by both supervisors and front-line employees. Because work expectations have expanded, some employees have legitimate reasons for raising this issue. They can honestly feel that additional responsibilities would pose a severe hardship, even if they believe that it is worthwhile for the organization as a whole to use S-OJT.

Needless to say, one should be extremely cautious about asking employees to become trainers if they are truly strained. Yet, until more is learned more about each situation, one cannot say whether this is true. First, when employees initially express their views about S-OJT, almost all say that it will probably take too much of their valuable work time. Can it be true that every minute of their workday is crammed with unrelenting activity? This cannot be accurate in all instances. Rather, it seems more likely that people naturally seek stability in their work lives and avoid any change, such as S-OJT, that could disrupt that stability.

Second, a trainer may become disgruntled when his or her supervisor does not provide sufficient time off to deliver S-OJT. Management needs to face the problems involved in releasing valuable employees to conduct the training. Long-term benefits should be carefully balanced against immediate needs. The point is that the organization should be willing to incur some reasonable costs, such as additional staff costs or slightly lowered production goals, to allow S-OJT to occur.

Third, after delivering S-OJT several times, many employees realize that S-OJT does not interfere with their on-going work activities as much as they had anticipated. In practice, trainers find both that S-OJT is delivered only once in a while and that it can be scheduled at mutually convenient times. In fact, some trainers—often those who voiced the loudest objections initially—look forward to the training as a way of breaking up their days and helping make their work more interesting.

Finally, some employees who express this issue about the lack of time, especially supervisors, are disingenuous. Traditionally, supervisors have been expected to develop their people. Nevertheless, until recently, others within the organization have borne much of this responsibility. In many instances, the organization's human resource development function has unwittingly taken over development activities that rightfully belong to supervisors and managers. Using S-OJT reminds supervisors that employee development programs are their responsibility, even if the organization has not held them accountable for it in the past.

Unwillingness to Train

The next issue—the unwillingness of some experienced employees to train others—is related to the first. Overcoming this unwillingness is one of the issues most often expressed regarding S-OJT. The stubborn refusal of these individuals can be extremely frustrating for managers seeking to implement

S-OJT. Unfortunately, it is virtually impossible to use S-OJT successfully without involving them.

There are two ways of responding to this issue. First, people have reasons for their actions, although the nature of this rationality is not always clear. A person's unwillingness to train is a product of either *organization-based reasons*—

- Fear of a loss of status as experts
- Fear of threatened job security
- Belief that it is not part of one's job to train others
- Absence of incentives for doing the extra work
- Mistrust of management's motives

—*or person-based reasons*—

- Discomfort in talking in front of others
- Uncertainty about what one knows
- Never having done anything like this before
- Lacking basic skills
- Nearing retirement age or will soon leave the organization for other reasons
- Fear of ridicule from peers

The challenge for management is to identify the reason in the particular situation at hand and then act accordingly. In general, if the reasons are organization based, employees should at least be made aware that, if the training is successful, the performance of the group training can improve. Thus, they have a stake in its success. For some employees, that is all that it takes to change their minds. In contrast, when the reasons are person based, the employee should be approached in a sensitive manner to determine whether he or she wants to address the feelings or deficiencies. Person-based reasons are usually the most difficult ones to deal with.

Second, one can question whether the issue is valid in the first place. While individuals have been encountered who were unwilling to train others, that fact has never affected the success or failure of S-OJT in their organization. If some employees do not want to train, then it is best to find employees who do. The fact that these other employees may be less knowledgeable in the work can be offset by the fact that they are interested in serving as trainers. In the long run, the second criterion could be more important than the first.

Experience suggests that most employees are in fact willing and interested to share what they know and can do with others. Of course, management may need to court and reassure some employees. But few employees ever refuse outright. In fact, some employees become trainers because they want to learn more about their area. For them, becoming a trainer is a way of satisfying their own learning needs. Management's expectation that employees will selfishly hoard their knowledge may be no more than a reflection of more traditional, less optimistic views of employees.

Trainers' Work Expectations

Chapter 10 discussed the importance of the organizational context for evaluating S-OJT. One aspect of the organizational context is management's willingness to change the work expectations of employees who serve as S-OJT trainers. It may not be possible for management to implement some changes entirely on its own initiative. For example, labor–management contracts may inhibit managers from changing work expectations without the full cooperation and agreement of their union partners. And even when changes are possible, it will doubtless take time for the change to become a permanent part of the organization. Nevertheless, the continuing effectiveness of S-OJT depends on a thorough review of trainer's work expectations.

Consider the implications for the different categories of employees who serve as S-OJT trainers. If *supervisors* or *managers* are to be the trainers, then the organization should:

- ensure that they have the appropriate competence needed to deliver the S-OJT,
- explicitly include the delivery of S-OJT in management's job descriptions,
- develop an easy-to-use system that allows managers to document and report the training progress of trainees,
- make the expectation to deliver training part of the performance reviews conducted by senior managers, and
- develop a system that gives managers periodic feedback on the quality of the training that they provide.

If *front-line employees* are to be the trainers, then the organization should:

- ensure that employees have the appropriate competence to deliver the S-OJT,
- provide the resources needed to cover for the work missed while employees deliver training,
- explicitly include the delivery of S-OJT in employee's job descriptions,
- develop an easy-to-use system that allows employees document and report the training progress of trainees, and
- develop a system that provides employees periodic feedback on the quality of the training.

These expectations are important for ensuring the quality of S-OJT.

Employee Development

Another issue that typically arises is the relationship between employee development and S-OJT. Chapter 2 described the four ways in which S-OJT can be used. Each way assumes that S-OJT is part of a larger employee development effort. Employee development is the planned process of using training and education to help individuals meet the organization's present and future needs (Jacobs & Washington, 2001; Jones & Jacobs, 1994). More and more organizations are recognizing that employee development systems are an essential part of their total quality programs. Continuous training and education opportunities help employees make use of all of their abilities and talents to perform their work (Vaught, Hoy, & Buchanan, 1985).

Unfortunately, S-OJT has sometimes been conducted without considering the individual needs of employees. Employees must feel that the training is moving them to a useful goal. Moreover, even when an organization has an employee development system, the system is often applied in a passive manner by management. That is, employees typically select training and educational experiences on their own without the guidance of a supervisor or knowledgeable advisor.

In more than one organization, S-OJT has led to the use of a more encompassing employee development system. One unanticipated effect of S-OJT is that it forces supervisors and managers to take a more active role in the development of their people.

Other Forms of Training in the Work Setting

An interesting counterpoint to S-OJT has been the growing literature on workplace training programs that seek to develop greater self-directedness and general problem-solving skills among trainees. De Jong (1991), whose research was conducted in the Netherlands, called this approach *on-site study*. Marsick, Cederholm, Turner, and Pearson (1992) refer to it as *action-reflection learning* (ARL). The underlying basis of these programs is that discovery learning, problem solving, and critical thinking should be the primary learning goals for trainees.

In practice, the training programs that use this approach take one of two forms: formal sessions conducted in the workplace or training embedded in the employee's work activities. Marsick and her colleagues state that action-reflection learning programs include the following:

- Employees working in small groups to solve problems
- Employees learning how to learn and think critically
- Employees identifying the skills needed to meet the requirements posed by the current work
- Employees developing a personal theory of management, leadership, or empowerment

The point seems evident that views of workplace training other than S-OJT have emerged. Clearly, competing approaches are not desirable. Each approach to workplace training seems to have its own strengths and weaknesses. Proponents of action-reflection learning suggest that it is most suitable when the problems at hand are especially complex and there are no immediate solutions in sight. Creative solutions based on the learning of individual group members can be the behavioral outcomes of action–reflection learning programs (Marsick, 1988). In contrast, S-OJT involves the learning by individuals who seek to attain pre-specified behavioral outcomes.

Possibly the most noticeable difference between S-OJT and action-reflection learning programs is the role of the trainer. Experienced employees are crucial in the design and delivery of S-OJT. For action-reflection learning programs, they play a different role: learning rather than source of work information. The reliance on experienced employees is said to put trainees at risk of becoming dependent on them and not seeking their own creative solutions to problems.

Clearly, S-OJT and action-reflection learning represent two fundamentally different perspectives on the training and learning process. In a practical sense, it seems less important to determine which is superior than it does to understand both thoroughly. Each approach can make sound contributions to organizational performance. However, the linkage between organizational outcomes and action-reflection learning programs is less clear than the linkage between organizational outcomes and S-OJT.

Use of the Deductive Method

Another issue of concern is related to the issue of competing approaches. That is, S-OJT has been perceived as a deductive methodology: The trainer presents the training content to the trainee, the trainee learns the content, and the trainee responds in a way that matches the presentation as closely as possible. The trainee seems to have few opportunities to internalize the content in ways other than that presented by the trainer.

While the deductive method is appropriate in many training situations, it is not appropriate in all situations. In fact, the use of inductive, or guided discovery, training is sometimes appropriate. Resembling action-reflection learning programs in some respects, the inductive method requires the trainee learn the content through his or her own discovery and problem-solving efforts.

In the past few years, interest in this issue has led to developing new forms of S-OJT. For example, a health care organization is using S-OJT organized by the guided discovery method with new newly promoted supervisors (Jacobs, 2002). The training program asks trainees to identify the mission of the organization and the four core values of the organization. The S-OJT is conducted by experienced supervisors or managers in the role of a facilitator. The trainer provides the training module and explains what should be done to achieve the training objectives. The trainer reviews strategic documents describing specific information. Then, the trainees conduct interviews with other experienced supervisors and managers according to a planned interview protocol. The purpose of the interview is to generate examples of the core values. The trainee documents this information in the S-OJT module. Finally, trainee and trainer review and discuss the information that has been documented. Of special importance, this training method enables trainees to generate positive and negative examples from direct observations close to their own work areas. These personal experiences help more than the previous classroom-based training approach to make them aware of the organization's intent and of the difficulties that employees face in carrying out that intent.

Role of HRD Staff

The last issue of concern is the proper role of HRD staff in the use of S-OJT. Clearly, there is much to do when S-OJT is used. HRD staff are uniquely suited to fulfill the following functions:

- Serve as the primary change agents by introducing S-OJT into the organization themselves or by bringing in external consultants.

- Provide technical assistance in many, if not all, aspects of the S-OJT process.

- Maintain files of the S-OJT modules and coordinate their revision.

- Coordinate the documentation of employee development plans.

Despite the many ways in which HRD staff can contribute, they still might feel left out of the process, since the S-OJT approach pushes the training process more directly onto the line side of the organization. Some HRD staff may resent that the training process seems to be out of their control. They may also be concerned that the success of S-OJT will leave senior management wondering why the organization needs an HRD function.

In a practical sense, HRD staff must not believe that their existence in the organization depends on their delivering off-the-job training programs. Instead, they must come to realize that their role is to develop employee competence to the appropriate levels with whatever means possible. To this end, HRD staff should think of themselves broadly as system designers, not narrowly as trainers or training designers. S-OJT has the potential to force HRD employees to reflect what their role has been in the past and on what it should be in the future if they are to make a meaningful contribution to their organization.

CONCLUSION

Change management and S-OJT are two different processes. The S-OJT process ensures that training will be designed, delivered, and evaluated in the most effective way possible. The change management process ensures that the organization will accept the S-OJT. The two processes should be used in combination to ensure the successful use of S-OJT. This final chapter has discussed seven issues of concern that are often raised when the use of S-OJT is considered: undue time burden, unwillingness to train, trainer's work expectations, employee development, other forms of training in the work setting, use of the deductive method, and the role of HRD staff.

Chapter 15
Conclusion: Developing a Culture of Expertise

At this point, the reader should understand the foundations of S-OJT, as well as know the S-OJT process. Finally, the reader should know the various ways to use S-OJT. This chapter concludes the book with an appeal for the development of a culture of expertise in organizations and society. S-OJT would likely play a major role in the development of such a culture.

A CULTURE OF EXPERTISE

While the primary aim of this book has been to provide a practical guide to S-OJT, the reader should also take away more than this information alone. As the title makes clear, the underlying rationale for the use of S-OJT is the need to develop individuals to the highest level of competence possible in a way that is both efficient and effective. Often, this means helping individuals develop the abilities of experts. Thus, the reader should begin to appreciate that expertise is not only a goal for individuals and organizations but also a goal for societies.

Managers can do many things to improve their organizations. They can bring in advanced technologies, streamline production and service delivery processes, introduce new products and services, and change work rules dramatically. In the same way, government leaders can take many different approaches to improve the lot of the people they represent. But when all is said and done, what variables ultimately determine the success of such efforts is the abilities of individuals.

With the past few years, numerous writers have proposed the *learning organization* and lifelong learning as metaphors for the way in which organizations and societies should undertake their own improvement and renewal (Watkins & Marsick, 1993; Marquardt & Sung, 2002). Of course, it is not organizations or societies that actually learn but rather the people within them. The learning organization gives employees the opportunity and license to explore their work environments fully on a continuous basis, and employees respond by accepting the need for change and initiating change on their own. Lifelong learning is important as it reinforces the general awareness that understanding the latest information is critical for success in a changing society.

The learning organization and lifelong learning concepts are attractive to managers and leaders who are searching for a model of the type of organization and society that they would like to create. Indeed, many organizations have adopted the position of chief learning officer instead of director of human resource development to demonstrate commitment to this vision.

However, one essential element is missing from the learning organization and lifelong learning models. Learning is important, but what can be done with the learning is equally if not even more important. In this same way, organization and societal leaders should value the accomplishments that result from learning as much as they value learning itself. While learning is a valued behavior, what organizations and societies also require is a *culture of expertise*.

For the good of both the organization and the individuals in it, individuals should be encouraged to engage in continuous learning activities—but not at the expense of forgetting that learning and doing go hand in hand. On the one hand, learning by itself does not lead to enhanced productivity or improved profitability. On the other hand, high levels of competence can be attained only through learning. Thus, having a learning organization and lifelong learning is a prerequisite to having a culture of expertise.

A culture of expertise is an environment—whether in an organization or society—that values what is done with the learning as much as it values the learning process itself. Managers and leaders have ultimate accountability for making such an environment possible.

Specifically, organization managers and leaders should consider the following four activities to bring about a culture of expertise:

1. Encourage individuals and groups to generate useful information that can help achieve important goals.

2. Establish systems that make it possible to document and store the useful information so that individuals and groups can call upon it when they need it.

3. Find ways of disseminating the useful information throughout the organization, in ways that are both efficient and effective.

4. Remove barriers and align consequences so that individuals and groups can be recognized and even celebrated for their high levels of competence.

S-OJT AND THE CULTURE OF EXPERTISE

S-OJT can play a helpful role in making a culture of expertise possible. In the most obvious sense, it provides a reliable way of disseminating important information to individuals, quickly and flexibly. Perhaps not so obvious are the ways in which S-OJT can make valuable contributions to other management activities.

For example, analyzing the work to be learned often brings insights into ways of performing the work better. Training modules can be used as a way of documenting and storing the information for purposes other than training. Finally, an organization can recognize experienced employees who serve as S-OJT trainers. All these contributions give S-OJT a key role in the culture of expertise. Viewed from this perspective, S-OJT can be seen as helping an organization and societies start the process of becoming a learning organization in the truest sense of the term, since it gives them a way of sharing old and new areas of know-how effectively and efficiently.

CONCLUSION

Organizations in the global economy realize that high levels of employee competence, or expertise, is a vital and dynamic living treasure. The desire to attain this level of competence is meaningless unless an organization and a society can develop it in ways that respond to its needs. S-OJT is one proven way of developing employee expertise that helps meet the changing demands of today's global economy.

Appendix A

Excerpts from the *Training within Industry Report* Describing the Lens Grinder Study

Chapter 2 (Excerpted): A CLEARINGHOUSE FOR INDUSTRIAL EXPERIENCE

TWI's early assistance to plants was largely of an advisory and consulting nature. This included surveys, either in an industry or of a particular plant, and the collecting and circulating of information about proven in-plant techniques. TWI, as one of the first emergency groups, was also frequently called on to collect information from contractors for the government and to influence war contractors to cooperate with other government agencies or accept other government policies. This latter stemmed out of the make-up of the TWI organization—local industrial people who had standing in the community.

The "Lens Grinder" Study

During the very first week of TWI's existence and while it still was a two-man organization of Director and Associate Director, the first assignment was received. All through the summer there had been much discussion of shortages in particular lines of skilled polishers for government arsenals and navy yards. This problem was presented to the TWI Directors and on August 28, 1940, they called to a conference on lens-grinding and precision instruments representatives of Sperry Gyroscope Corporation, Leeds & Northrup, Bausch and Lomb, General Electric Company, Eastman Kodak Company, who met with staff members of the National Defense Commission and representatives of Army and Navy Ordnance and Frankford Arsenal.

As a result of this conference, TWI arranged to borrow M. J. Kane from American Telephone and Telegraph to make plant visits and write the material in training form.

The original problem in the lens-grinding field was to assist government arsenals and navy yards to get 350 properly qualified lens grinders. It was considered that a qualified learner did well to master the art of lens-grinding in five years. Upon studying the problem, it was found that 20 jobs are really included in lens-grinding. It had been assumed that a lens-grinder must be able to perform all 20 jobs. In the emergency, the specific solution recommended was to upgrade workers then employed on precision optical work to the most highly skilled jobs, and to break in new people on just one of the simplest jobs. This required production specifications and intensive training.

Key Points

Experimental work was done by E. A. Fricke of Frankford Arsenal and Mr. Kane, at the Frankford Arsenal, the Bausch & Lomb Optical Company, and the Eastman Kodak Company. One kind of work was found to include 14 operations. Each of these operations was broken down by an experienced worker into segments and made full-time work since the volume of production warranted it. Each part of the job was studied to find the important features. Out of this experience grew the conception of "key points." This practical discovery was destined to lift job instruction to an entirely new level of usefulness.

Much of this supposedly difficult work was relatively simple and easy. A few critical points determined whether the whole operation was successful. Furthermore, it was possible to isolate these critical points. These points were the keys to good work and the keys to good lenses, and these were soon referred to as "key points." Thus was born a phrase and a conception that some months later was to form the cornerstone of a nation-wide production training effort.

The Instruction Process

Careful thought was also given to the process of instruction itself by which a lens-grinding operation, with its key points, could be put over to the learner. Based on the instruction steps developed by C. R. Allen in World War I, the following method was recommended by Mr. Kane:

1. Show him how to do it
2. Explain the key points
3. Let him watch you do it again
4. Let him do the simple parts of the job
5. Help him do the whole job
6. Let him do the whole job—but watch him
7. Put him on his own

In November 1940 these steps, along with the "key points" idea, were incorporated in a bulletin, "Helping the Experienced Worker Break in a Man on a New Job."

In an account of this experiment, "A Study of Lens Grinding," it was stated:

The main purpose in having the worker identify these key points is to enable him to recall them when he is breaking in new people. His own familiarity with the work often causes a competent worker to overlook the difficulties he had during his early stages and thus without intention, he fails to mention these difficulties when breaking in a new man.

It was also found that the production sequence was not always the best learning order.

TWI thought that, by this demonstration, and by using the specific steps outlined in its instruction bulletin, a plant could break down its own skilled jobs. This stress on the value of key points and of taking small instruction steps one at a time, plus the outlining of a method of good instruction, was expected to equip plants to go ahead on their own.

Completing the Cycle

As a result of this work, the training of people for the separate jobs involved in lens-grinding was reduced from approximately five years to a matter of months. Everyone—the arsenals and plants as well as TWI—was well satisfied. Experience was to prove however that these principles had not been milked dry. In the summer of 1945 a TWI field man reported that a TWI-trained man in a lens plant had been assigned the job of reducing the four to six months that it then took before a new man "made production."

The plant's training department had never been able to break in on this territory because it was considered sacred by those in charge—none of these newfangled ideas for them! Management decided to set up a new department in a different building and use all new help—workers from another department (which had been terminated) who had never done any lens-grinding. A job instructor was trained, and three men were assigned to him on a test basis. By the end of the first day all three had ground satisfactory lenses— without any scrap whatsoever! It was estimated that in 6 weeks' time over 100 persons would be working in this department and all of them would be "making production."

Advisory Commission to the Council of National Defense

Labor Division

"Training within Industry"   Practice Report #1

A STUDY OF LENS GRINDING

The Problem

Early in the fall of 1940 a shortage of properly qualified lens grinders made itself apparent. An immediate call for 350 qualified lens grinders for work in government arsenals and navy yards placed on the Government Service and Civil Service failed to locate skilled men.

The additional 350 lens grinders were needed because an expanded defense production program called for precision optical instruments greatly in excess of anything like normal production quantities.

After the unsuccessful search for properly qualified lens grinders, some alternative had to be worked out because these instruments had to be delivered. It was found that the term *lens grinder* means very little because within this classification of work there is a wide range of skills covering a number of different precision optical operations. The fully competent lens grinder, like the first-class machinist, is supposed to be able to do successfully any job that falls in the classification. The following list covers the work done by the fully competent lens grinder:

1. Cut optical glass
2. Grind lenses
3. Grind prisms
4. Grind reticles
5. Grind windows or covers
6. Correct prisms for polish
7. Blocking prisms

8. Blocking reticles

9. Silvering (ordinary)

10. Silvering (oculars & cutting)

11. Etching (special)

12. Etching (general)

13. Polishing (prism blocks)

14. Polishing small lenses

15. Polishing large lenses

16. Polishing repairs

17. Centering

18. Cementing (lens)

19. Cementing (ocular prisms)

20. Roof prisms (correction)

The most commonsense alternative was to explore the possibility of "upgrading" workers now employed on precision optical work to more skilled jobs and "breaking in" workers who had relatively low skill or no skill at all on the simple parts of the work with the idea of quickly perfecting their production ability on one part. Thus, by specializing the work and giving thought to intensive training of present workers as well as new men on parts of the production of lenses, it seemed possible to get out volume production without developing all workers to all-around skill.

What Was Done

A group of competent supervisors and workmen employed at the Frankford Arsenal in Philadelphia, the Bausch and Lomb Optical Company at Rochester, and the Eastman Kodak Company at Rochester, selected for study one type of precision optical instrument that would embrace nearly all the skills required of a fully competent lens grinder. For this purpose, the production of the M-1 Circle Aiming instrument was chosen and it embraces the following operations:

1. Cut glass
2. Block lenses for grinding
3. Grind lenses
4. Edge-grind reticles
5. Grind poro prisms
6. Grind compass covers
7. Block prisms for polishing
8. Block reticles for polishing
9. Block lenses for finish grinding
10. Block polishing (prisms and reticles)
11. Etching reticles
12. Lens polishing
13. Lens centering
14. Cementing lenses

The Analysis of Operations

These operations in turn were broken down by experienced workers into job assignments which, while only part of the completed operation, could provide full-time employment for a new worker if the volume of production warranted it. After setting up these job assignments or specialized parts of the production, each was studied with the thought of determining the one or two important features or "key points" which when mastered help the new worker learn how to do the work.

Looking over the list of key points included in this study, it will be noticed that they are not always susceptible of written explanation. Experience proves that they can be *definitely identified* by the experienced worker. In this study it was not thought necessary in every case to provide a written description of the knack, special movements, or particular information identified as key points. The main purpose in having the worker identify these key points is to enable

CHART #1 PORO PRISMS	
Sequence in Which Work Must be Done	*Sequence for Upgrading*
1. Grind one side (individually by hand)	1. Grind one side (individually by hand)
2. Block on piano tool preparatory to grinding for thickness	2. Remove from block and clean
3. Grind to thickness	3. Block on piano tool
4. Remove and clean grinding	4. Block for hypotenuse
5. Block prisms for grinding 90° angles	5. Block prisms for 90° angles
6. Grind two 90° angles	6. Bevel edges
7. Block for hypotenuse grinding	7. Grind to thickness
8. Grind hypotenuse	8. Grind hypotenuse
9. Grind top level	9. Grind top level
10. Grind ends to size	10. Grind ends to size
11. Rough radius (lathe)	11. Grind two 90° angles
12. Fit by hand to gauge	12. Grind radius (lathe)
13. Bevel	13. Fit to gauge by hand
14. Hand correction	14. 45° angle
	15. Hand correction

him to recall them when he is breaking in new people. His own familiarity with the work often causes the competent worker to overlook the difficulties he had during the early stages and thus without intention he fails to mention these difficulties and how to overcome them when breaking in a new man.

It was also found that the order or sequence with which work must be done for production is not always the best sequence for growth in skill. These separate skills, forming the total skill of a fully competent man, are best acquired in a series of progressive steps. If a new man can be given these successive assignments and masters the key points, he will eventually become fully competent as a lens grinder. Three production units are used as an illustration and these are set up first in the order or sequence in which it is best to assign new people for quick learning. Following these lists are the detailed breakdowns of some of the job assignments. The production units are Poro Prisms, Lenses and Reticles as required for the M-1 Circle Aiming instrument.

Conclusion
As a direct result of this study, a simple pattern for recording an analysis of production jobs was worked out. In addition, some short instructions for an experienced worker to follow in teaching "production jobs" were designed.

The pattern has been applied in two shops manufacturing precision optical products. It has been tried out in a small way by industries making other defense products. The evidence so far indicates that the pattern can be used successfully to "break in" new workers rapidly. Of course, the specific application of such a pattern must fit local requirements. In general there are two types of training situations to be met in the defense program:

1. Training in an organization that is now engaged in defense production and finds its defense contracts require an increase of workers greatly in excess of normal growth;

2. Training in an organization that is undertaking to make a product that is an entirely different one from its regular production activity.

In the first situation it is not necessary as a general rule to develop new production routines or methods. It is necessary to prepare the supervisors so that they can carry out the actual training required. A beginning can easily be made on this by starting with a few supervisors, who have indicated their interest in training and who will assist in preparing an outline of a sufficient number of their jobs to form a progressive series for upgrading. The supervisors selected to work out the training pattern do not necessarily have to cover the production jobs for which training is most essential. It is desirable to have a good example of the pattern worked out because the support of the supervisory force is best obtained through having them convince themselves that through the use of the pattern of this sort they will eliminate many of the production difficulties. It is well to start with the simpler jobs because when they have prepared and the usefulness of the pattern in training has been demonstrated, it will be easier to convince the supervisor who has the real problem in breaking new employees that this approach will aid him in meeting his responsibilities.

In such a procedure it is well to assign a staff employee as assistant to the supervisor in making the analysis of the job and in making the training outline. Such a staff employee should be familiar in a general way with the processes involved and should have an inquisitive, or exploratory, type of mind that will ferret out the "key points" involved in doing the work.

In the second situation where the organization is entering into the production of an entirely new product, the first step toward the development of such a pattern is made when the engineer breaks the product down into the operations involved for estimating purposes. The next step involves the development and setting up of the first trial method for doing the work in each of the process steps. When the methods to be used are worked out they should be in enough detail so that they can be used for training purposes.

An effective method of building the necessary organization is to take from the existing organization, or from the outside, a nucleus of new employees who have had experience in such, or similar, work or who can be trained quickly. Then using the breakdown that the industrial engineers have prepared, start this smaller group of employees out on the prescribed methods. While the method is being developed in this manner by the experienced employees under the guidance of the regular supervisor with the assistance of the industrial engineer, the key points that must be imparted to the new operator can be developed and added to the steps of the process laid down by the engineers. Thus when the skeleton organization, which is to serve as trainers of the new employees as they are brought in, has finished its training period and the initial layout of method has been revised as found by trial, actual training of the new workers can begin.

The attached exhibit is intended to show the difference in sequence between the learning assignment of operations and the order in which they must be carried out for production.

Exhibit A shows the production order for the product selected. Exhibit A-1 shows the learning sequence or the order in which operations should be assigned for progressive growth in skill or knowledge.

It will be noticed on Exhibit A-1 that progression factors have been selected in order to properly place each operation in sequence so that each one makes a demand for an increased ability on one or more of the factors shown.

Of course, for a different product a different set of progression factors will have to be chosen, and these must be determined for the product and agreed on by the firm setting up the sequence.

M. J. Kane
Training Consultant
Washington, D.C.
March 15, 1941

EXHIBIT A Production Order of Jobs, PORO PRISMS

Operation #1	Grind one side (individually by hand)
Operation #2	Block on plane tool preparatory to grinding for thickness
Operation #3	Grind to thickness
Operation #4	Remove and clean
Operation #5	Block prisms for grinding 90° angles
Operation #6	Grind two 90° angles
Operation #7	Block for hypotenuse grinding
Operation #8	Grind hypotenuse
Operation #9	Grind top level
Operation #10	Grind ends to size
Operation #11	Rough radius (lathe)
Operation #12	Fit by hand to gauge
Operation #13	Bevel
Operation #14	Hand correction

EXHIBIT A-1   Sample Training Sequence of Jobs for Making Optical Glass Poro Prisms

These separate jobs are arranged in the order best suited for training a man successive assignments, on each of which he will develop more skill and knowledge on one or more of the progress factors as shown.

Operations are to be assigned in numerical order from #1 Fully trained man	.0001″ and fractions of min- utes on angles	Color Test Perfect	High- est	$15 per piece and up	Com- plex
15. Hand correction 14. 45° angle 13. Fit to gauge by hand 4th Level	↑	↑	↑	↑	↑
12. Grind radius (lathe) 11. Grind two 90° angles 10. Grind ends to size 9. Grind top bevel 3rd Level	Accuracy in working to dimensions	Quality of surface produced	Care required in handling finished surfaces	Increased value due to previous processing	Set-up—Adjusting equipment
8. Grind hypotenuse 7. Grind to thickness 6. Bevel edges 5. Block prisms for 90° angles 2nd Level					
4. Block for hypote- nuse grinding 3. Block on plane tool 2. Remove from block and clean 1. Grind one size (hand) 1st Level					

Appendix B
S-OJT Trainer Evaluation Form

Trainer:	Observation Date:
Name/Dept.:	
Task Name:	
Evaluator:	
Location: __ Field __ Laboratory __ Simulator Other:	

Get Ready to Train

Specific training time scheduled with trainee	Approximate training time scheduled with trainee	Training time uncertain or not specified
1	2	3
Tools and equipment needed for the training reserved in advance and available for use	Tools and equipment needed for the training known and ready	Tools and equipment needed for missing or not known
1	2	3

Training materials sent to trainee with instructions	Training materials made available during training	Training materials incomplete or parts missing
1	2	3
Location reserved for training	Location identified during training	Location uncertain or not specified
1	2	3
Trainee's manager informed of the specific time and location	Trainee's manager aware that the training would occur	Trainee's manager unaware of the training
1	2	3

Prepare the Trainee

Purpose and rationale of the training clearly presented	Purpose and rationale of the training presented	Purpose and rationale of the training not presented
1	2	3
Trainee prerequisites clearly presented and confirmed	Trainee prerequisites presented and confirmed	Trainee prerequisites omitted or in error
1	2	3
General safety and quality requirements clearly presented	General safety and quality requirements presented	General safety and quality requirements omitted or in error
1	2	3
How the training will be done clearly presented	How the training will be done presented	How the training will be done omitted or in error
1	2	3
Trainee questions about the training solicited and answered clearly	Trainee questions about the training answered	Trainee questions about the training not solicited or answered in error
1	2	3

Present the Content

Trainer positioned the trainee during all training	Trainer positioned the trainee for some training	Trainer did not position the trainee or in error
1	2	3
Trainer covered all aspects of the overview	Trainer covered most aspects of the overview	Trainer omitted covering the overview or in error
1	2	3
Trainer presented all safety and quality points	Trainer presented most safety and quality points	Trainer omitted safety and quality points or in error
1	2	3
Trainer presented say and do for all components	Trainer presented say and do for most components	Trainer omitted say and do or some in error
1	2	3
Trainer presented appropriate examples	Trainer presented some examples	Trainer omitted examples or were incorrect
1	2	3
Trainer presented complete summary at end	Trainer presented summary at end	Trainer omitted summary or was incomplete
1	2	3

Require a Response

Trainer asked trainee to be in correct position	Trainer asked trainee to be in position	Trainer omitted asking to be in position or in error
1	2	3
Trainer asked the trainee to cover all aspects of the overview	Trainer asked trainee to present an overview	Trainer omitted asking for an overview or was in error
1	2	3

Trainer asked trainee to present all safety and quality points 1	Trainer asked trainee to present safety and quality points 2	Trainer omitted asking for safety and quality points or in error 3
Trainer asked trainee to say and do for all components 1	Trainer asked trainee to say and do components 2	Trainer omitted asking for say and do or in error 3
Trainer asked trainee to present and generate examples 1	Trainer asked trainee to present examples 2	Trainer omitted asking for examples or were incorrect 3
Trainer asked trainee to present complete summary 1	Trainer asked trainee to present summary 2	Trainer omitted asking for summary or in error 3

Provide Feedback

Trainer closely observed trainee during response 1	Trainer observed trainee during the response 2	Trainer failed to observe trainee during response 3
Trainer informed trainee about the correctness of the response at appropriate time 1	Trainer informed trainee about the correctness of response 2	Trainer failed to inform about correctness of response or in error 3
Trainer provided coaching for improvement 1	Trainer provided some coaching 2	Trainer failed to provide any coaching 3
Trainer asked and responded to all questions at appropriate times 1	Trainer asked and responded to questions 2	Trainer failed to ask questions or respond to questions or in error 3

Trainer pointed out all embedded cues	Trainer pointed out embedded cues	Trainer failed to point out embedded cues
1	2	3

Evaluate Performance

Trainer asked trainee for a self-report and included response in evaluation	Trainer asked trainee for a self-report	Trainer failed to ask trainee for self-report
1	2	3
Trainer rated trainee perform- ance accurately and reliably	Trainer rated trainee performance	Trainer failed to rate performance accurately or reliably
1	2	3
Trainer docu- mented trainee performance accurately and completely	Trainer docu- mented trainee performance	Trainer failed to document trainee performance accurately or completely
1	2	3

Overall Rating of the Session

_____ Satisfactory—All training events were rated at least 2

_____ Unsatisfactory—Any training event rated less than 2

Evaluator Comment:

Evaluator Signature:

Trainer Comment:

Trainer Signature:

Supervisor Comment:

Supervisor Signature:

Appendix C
Trainee Evaluation Form

Training Title: _____

Date of Training: _____

Trainer Name: _____

Time/Location of Training: _____

Before the Training Session

I knew the specific training time.	I knew the approximate training time.	I was uncertain of the training time.
1	2	3
I had the tools and equipment needed for the training.	I had most of the tools and equipment needed for the training.	I did not have any tools and equipment needed for the training.
1	2	3
I received the training materials well before the training.	I received the training materials before or during the training.	I did not have any of the training materials or parts missing.
1	2	3
I knew the specific training location in advance.	I knew the training location in advance.	I was uncertain of the training location.
1	2	3

My manager was informed of the training time in advance.	My manager was aware that the training would occur sometime.	My manager was unaware of the training.
1	2	3

Before the Training

I clearly understood the purpose and rationale of the training.	I understood the purpose and rationale of the training.	I did not understand the purpose and rationale of the training.
1	2	3
I was asked in depth if I had the prerequisites for the training.	I was asked if I had the prerequisites for the training.	I was not asked if I had the prerequisites for the training.
1	2	3
I learned about all general safety and quality requirements.	I learned about most general safety and quality requirements.	I did not learn about general safety and quality requirements.
1	2	3
I understood clearly how the training was to be done.	I understood how the training was to be done.	I did not understand how the training was to be done.
1	2	3
I was asked if I had questions and they were answered clearly.	I was asked whether I had any questions.	I was not asked if I had any questions or answered in error.
1	2	3

During the Training

I was positioned by the trainer throughout the training.	I was positioned by the trainer during most of the training.	I was not positioned by the trainer or in error.
1	2	3
I received a complete overview of the training content.	I received an overview of the training content.	I did not receive an overview of the training content or in error.
1	2	3
I learned about all specific safety and quality points.	I learned about most safety and quality points.	I did not learn about specific safety and quality points.
1	2	3
I was shown and heard about each training component.	I was shown and heard about most training components.	I was not shown or heard about any training components.
1	2	3
I was given several examples that seemed relevant to the training.	I was given some examples relevant to the training.	I was not given any examples or were ones given not relevant.
1	2	3
II received a complete summary at the end.	I received a summary at the end.	I did not receive a summary or it was incomplete.
1	2	3

During Practice Time

I was asked always to be in correct position.	I was asked to be in correct position.	I was not asked to be in correct position or in error.
1	2	3
I was asked to give a complete overview of the training.	I was asked to give an overview of the training.	I was not asked to give an overview of the training.
1	2	3
I was asked to state all safety and quality points.	I was asked to state safety and quality points.	I was not asked to state safety and quality points or in error.
1	2	3
I was asked to say and do for all components.	It was suggested that I say and do for the training components.	I was not asked to say and do any of the training components.
1	2	3
I was asked to repeat examples and new ones if possible.	I was asked to repeat examples that were given.	I was not asked to repeat examples or generate new ones.
1	2	3
I was asked to present a complete summary of the content.	I was asked to present a summary of the content.	I was not asked to present a summary.
1	2	3

Feedback During Practice

I was closely observed during my practice time.	I was observed during most of my practice time.	I was not observed during any of my practice time.
1	2	3

I was informed about the correctness of all my responses.	I was informed about the correctness of most responses.	I was not informed about the correctness of any responses.
1	2	3
I received coaching throughout my practice time.	I received some coaching during my practice time.	I did not receive any coaching during my practice time.
1	2	3
I received answers to all my questions.	I received answers to most of my questions.	I did not receive any answers or answered in error.
1	2	3
I learned about all the embedded cues in the work setting.	I learned some embedded cues in the work setting.	I did not learn about any embedded cues.
1	2	3

My Performance

I was asked and probed whether I understood the content.	I was asked whether I understood the content.	I was not asked whether I understood the training.
1	2	3
My trainer's rating accurately represented my learning.	My trainer's rating was more or less accurate of my learning.	My trainer did not rate my learning accurately.
1	2	3
My trainer recorded my rating information exactly as told to me.	My trainer recorded my rating as told to me.	My trainer recorded my rating differently from what I was told.
1	2	3

Overall Rating of the Session

____ Satisfactory—All training events were rated at least 2

____ Unsatisfactory—Any training event rated less than 2

Trainee's Comment:

Trainee's Signature:

Appendix D
Sample S-OJT Module with Embedded Training Events

Title: **Responding to Guest Complaints**

INTRODUCTION

1. Prepare the trainee

Present the title of the module and talk through purpose and rationale as presented in the module.

Emphasize the importance of guest relations as part of the overall corporate mission to increase competitiveness and reduce costs.

Review how the training will be done. Explain that you expect the trainee to review the module before-hand. The training location should be the front desk area.

The manner in which GSRs handle a guest complaint is one of the most important factors that will determine our success in the 1990s.

Why? A recent study reported that 95% of guests who complain will do business with a company again if their complaint is resolved quickly and fairly.

You may feel that responding to complaints is one of the least pleasant parts of your job. However, complaints are actually GOOD NEWS! They are an opportunity to save the relationship between the guest and the company.

As you listen to the guest complaining, it's natural to think,

"Why is she upset with me? It's not my fault. Probably someone else created the problem."

or

"The guest is overreacting! The problem is not that big a deal."

or

"If the guest is going to be rude to me, then I'm going to be rude right back."

These thoughts can lead to negative attitudes and get in the way of solving the problem. Sooner or later, negative attitudes come across to the guest in the form of a frown, rolling eyes, or tone of voice.

Ask the trainee whether he or she has any experiences in dealing with guest complaints.

Do you have experiences in reacting this way?

WHAT YOU WILL LEARN

2. Present the content

Make sure you arrange the front desk area so that you and the trainee face each other. Make sure that there will be few interruptions.

Training should be stopped immediately if a guest enters the lobby.

After completing this module, you will be able to:

1. understand what is a guest complaint,

2. identify common types of guest complaints, and

3. use our *Complaint Response Process (CRP)* to resolve guest complaints.

OVERVIEW OF THE CRP

2. Present the training

Present an overview of the CRP making sure that you state each step and provide a brief summary of its meaning.

Generate examples or use the one given in the module. Ask the trainee to generate a scenario that you can apply.

Read through the example, then discuss how the GSR might use the steps to address the real issue.

This training will help you use the CRP. The CRP helps create a win-win outcome for the guest and the company.

The CRP has seven steps:

1. Actively listen.

2. Ask for details.

3. Document guest comments.

4. Acknowledge guest concerns.

5. Reference company policies.

6. Identify possible solutions.

7. Take action and follow up.

Here's a situation in which the CRP can be used.

It's 7 P.M. and the GM has left for the day. A guest enters the lobby and says, "Don't you ever pick up the phone?"

How does this approach compare to your approach?

Let's look at what we mean by a customer complaint and then we'll go through each step of the CRP.

References

Al-Muzaini, B. S., Al-Keane, A., & Al-Awadi, S. (2002). Transitioning from unstructured to structured on-the-job training. In R. L. Jacobs (Ed.), *Implementing on-the-job learning* (pp. 183–189). Alexandria, VA: American Society for Training and Development.

Aring, M. (1998). *The teaching firm: Where productive work and learning converge: Report on research findings and implications.* Newton, MA: Center for Workforce Development, Education Development Center, Inc.

Ausubel, D. P. (1968). *Educational psychology: A cognitive view.* New York: Holt, Rinehart & Winston.

Baldridge National Quality Program. (2002). Technology Division, Department of Commerce: Washington, D.C. Available: www.quality.nist.gov/.

Baldwin, T. T., & Ford, K. J. (1988). Transfer of training: A review and directions for future research. *Personnel Psychology, 41*(1), 63–105.

Bandura, A. (1978). *Social learning theory.* Englewood Cliffs, NJ: Prentice Hall.

Bierema, L., Bing, J., & Carter, T. (2002). The global pendulum. *Training and Development,* 70–78.

Billesbach, T. (1991). A study of the implementation of just in time in the U.S. *Production and Inventory Management Journal, 32*(3), 1–4.

Black, D., & Bottenberg, R. A. (1973). *Comparison of technical school and on-the-job training as methods of skill up-grading.* San Antonio, TX: Air Force Human Resources Laboratory.

Bloom, B. S. (1984). The 2-sigma problem: The search for methods of group instruction as effective as one-on-one tutoring. *Educational Researcher, 13*(6), 4–16.

Brinkerhoff, R. O. (1987). *Achieving results from training: How to evaluate human resource development to strengthen programs and increase impact.* San Francisco: Jossey-Bass.

Broad, M. L., & Newstrom, J. W. (1992). *Transfer of training: Action-packed strategies to ensure higher payoffs from training investments.* Reading, MA: Addison-Wesley.

Broadwell, M. M. (1986). *The supervisor and on-the-job training.* Reading, MA: Addison-Wesley.

Brown, C., & Reich, M. (2002). *Developing skills and pay through career ladders: Lessons from Japanese and U.S. companies.* Berkeley: Institute of Industrial Relations, University of California, Berkeley.

Brown, J. S., Collins, A., & Duguid, P. (1989). Situated cognition and the culture of learning. *Educational Researcher, 18*(1), 32–41.

Carlisle, K. E. (1986). *Analyzing jobs and tasks.* Englewood Cliffs, NJ: Educational Technology Publications.

Carnevale, A. P. (1991). *America and the new economy.* Alexandria, VA: American Society for Training and Development and Employment Training Administration, U.S. Department of Labor.

Carnevale, A. P., & Gainer, L. J. (1989). *The learning enterprise.* Alexandria, VA: American Society for Training and Development and Employment and Training Administration, U.S. Department of Labor.

Carnevale, A. P., & Gainer, L. J. (1994). Trends in training on the job. *Technical and Skills Training,* 10–16.

Chaney, L. H., & Martin, J. S. (2000). *International business communication.* Englewood Cliffs, NJ: Prentice Hall.

Chi, M. T., Glaser, R., & Farr, M. J. (1988). *The nature of expertise.* Hillsdale, NJ: Erlbaum.

Churchill, G. A., Ford, N. M., & Walker, O. C. (1985). *Sales force management: Planning, implementation, and control.* Homewood, IL: Irwin.

Connor, J. (1983). *On-the-job training.* Boston: International Human Resources Development Corporation.

Cronbach, L. J., & Snow, R. E. (1977). *Aptitudes and instructional methods.* New York: Irvington.

Cummings, T. G., & Worley, C. G. (2001). *Organization development and change* (7th ed.). St. Paul, MN: West.

De Gram, C., & Glaude, M. (2000). *Structured on-the-job training: Design and implementation.* Hertogenbosch, The Netherlands: National Agency Leonardo da Vinci.

De Jong, J. A. (1991). The multiple forms of on-site training. *Human Resource Development Quarterly, 2*(4), 307–317.

De Jong, J. A. (1993). Structured on-the-job training at Hoogovens Ijmuiden. *Journal of European Industrial Training, 17*(2), 8–13.

De Jong, J. A., & Bogaards, L. (2002). Structured OJT in a changing organizational context: The Corus Steel Works at Ijmuiden, the Netherlands. In R. L. Jacobs (Ed.), *Implementing on-the-job learning* (pp. 73–85). Alexandria, VA: American Society for Training and Development.

De Jong, J. A., Thijssen, J. G. L., & Versloot, B. M. (2001). Planned training on the job: A typology. In R. L. Jacobs (Ed.), *Planned training on the job* (Vol. 3, Number 4, pp. 408–414). Thousand Oaks, CA: Sage.

Dehnbostel, P. (2001). Learning bays in German manufacturing companies. In R. L. Jacobs (Ed.), *Planned training on the job* (Vol. 3, Number 4, pp. 471–479). Thousand Oaks, CA: Sage.

Dixon, N. M. (1990). *Evaluation: A tool for improving HRD quality.* San Diego, CA: University Associates.

Dooley, C. R. (1945). *The Training within Industry report (1940–1945): A record of the development of supervision—Their use and the results.* Washington, D.C.: War Manpower Commission, Bureau of Training, Training within Industry Service.

Dowling, N. (1992). *The relationship between senior managers' quality management behaviors and subordinate managers' commitment to quality.* Unpublished doctoral dissertation, Ohio State University.

Drucker, P. (1993). *Post-capitalist society.* New York: HarperCollins.

EnterpriseOhio Network. (1998). *Success stories: Productivity improves through employee cross-training.* Available: www.enterpriseohio.org.

Fournies, F. F. (1978). *Coaching for improved work performance.* New York: Van Nostrand Reinhold.

Fry, L., & Barnard, J. (2002). Implementing an e-learning management system for call center employees. In R. L. Jacobs (Ed.), *Implementing on-the-job learning* (pp. 159–166). Alexandria, VA: American Society for Training and Development.

Futrell, C. (1988). *Sales management.* Hinsdale, IL: Dryden.

Gagne, R. M., Briggs, L. J., & Wager, W. W. (1988). *Principles of instructional design.* New York: Holt, Rinehart & Winston.

Galagan, P. (1990). David Kearns: A CEO's view of training. *Training and Development, 44*(5), 41–50.

Garrick, J. (1998). *Informal learning in the workplace: Unmasking human resource development.* London: Routledge.

Gilbert, T. F. (1978). *Human competence: Engineering worthy performance.* New York: McGraw-Hill.

Goldstein, I. (1974). *Training program development.* Monterey, CA: Brooks/Cole.

Gommersall, E., & Meyers, M. S. (1966). Breakthrough in on-the-job training. *Harvard Business Review, 44*(4), 62–72.

Goodman, P. S., & Dean, J. W. (1983). Why productivity efforts fail. In W. French, C. Dean, & R. Zawacki (Eds.), *Organization development: Theory, practice, and research.* Plano, TX: Business Publications.

Harless, J. H. (1978). *An ounce of analysis is worth a pound of objectives.* Newnan, GA: Harless Performance Guild.

Hart-Landsberg, S., Braunger, J., Reder, S., & Cross, M. M. (1992). *Learning the ropes: The social construction of work-based learning.* Berkeley, CA: National Center for Research in Vocational Education.

Hartley, J., & Davies, I. K. (1976). Preinstructional strategies: The role of pretests, behavioral objectives, overviews, and advance organizers. *Review of Educational Research, 46*(2), 239–265.

Hoerner, J., & Wehrley, J. (2000). *Work-based learning: The key to school-to-work transition.* New York: Glencoe.

Hoffman, H. (1997). Growing our own: On-the-job training in a local-government health department. In M. L. Broad (Ed.), *Transferring learning in the workplace* (pp. 57–70). Alexandria, VA: American Society for Training and Development.

Hofstede, Geert. H. (2001). *Culture's consequences: comparing values, behaviors, institutions, and organizations across nations.* Thousand Oaks, CA: Sage Publications, c2001.

International Organization for Standardization. (2000a). *ISO 9000, Quality management systems—Fundamentals and vocabulary (CHF104).* Geneva, Switzerland: Author.

International Organization for Standardization. (2000b). *Quality management system requirements: ISO 9001.* Geneva, Switzerland: Author. Available: www.iso.ch/.

Jacobs, R. L. (1986). Use of the critical incident technique to analyze the interpersonal skill requirements of supervisors. *Journal of Industrial Teacher Education, 23*(2), 56–61.

Jacobs, R. L. (1989). Systems theory applied to human resource development. In D. Gradous (Ed.), *Systems theory applied to human resource development*. Alexandria, VA: American Society for Training and Development.

Jacobs, R. L. (1990). Structured on-the-job training. In H. Stolovitch & E. Keeps (Eds.), *Handbook of human performance technology: A comprehensive guide for analyzing and solving performance problems in organizations*. San Francisco: Jossey-Bass.

Jacobs, R. L. (1994). Comparing the training efficiency and product quality of unstructured and structured OJT. In J. Phillips (Ed.), *The return on investment in human resource development: Cases on the economic benefits of HRD*. Alexandria, VA: American Society for Training and Development.

Jacobs, R. L. (Ed.). (2001). *Planned training on the job* (Vol. 3, Number 4). Thousand Oaks, CA: Sage.

Jacobs, R. L. (2002a). Institutionalizing organizational change through cascade training. *Journal of European Industrial Training, 26*(2/3/4), 177–182.

Jacobs, R. L. (2002b). Using structured on-the-job training to inform new supervisors of the organization's core values. In R. L. Jacobs (Ed.), *Implementing on-the-job learning* (pp. 97–110). Alexandria, VA: American Society for Training and Development.

Jacobs, R. L., & Hawley, J. (2002). *Defining workforce development and implications for graduate instruction: A report to the Workforce Development and Education faculty*. Columbus: Graduate Program in Workforce Development and Education, the Ohio State University.

Jacobs, R., & Hruby-Moore, M. (1998). Comparing the forecasted and actual financial benefits of human resource development programs: Learning from failure. *Performance Improvement Quarterly, 11*(2), 93–100.

Jacobs, R. L., Jones, M. J., & Neil, S. (1992). A case study in forecasting the financial benefits of unstructured and structured on-the-job training. *Human Resource Development Quarterly, 3*(2), 133–139.

Jacobs, R. L., & McGiffin, T. D. (1987). A human performance system using a structured on-the-job training approach. *Performance and Instruction, 25*(7), 8–11.

Jacobs, R. L., & Osman-Gani, A. M. (1999). Status, impact, and implementation issues of structured on-the-job training: A study of Singapore-based companies. *Human Resource Development International, 2*(1), 17–24.

Jacobs, R. L., & Russ-Eft, D. (2001). Cascade training and institutionalizing organizational change. In R. L. Jacobs (Ed.), *Planned training on the job* (Vol. 3, Number 4, pp. 496–503). Thousand Oaks, CA: Sage.

Jacobs, R. L., Russ-Eft, D., & Zidan, S. S. (2001). *Institutionalizing organizational change through cascade training: Implications for HRD research*. Paper presented at the Annual Conference of the Academy of Human Resource Development.

Jacobs, R., & Washington, C. (2003). Employee development and organizational performance: A review of literature and directions for future research. *Human Resource Development International, 6*(2).

Johnson, S. D., & Leach, J. A. (2001). Using expert employees to train on the job. In R. L. Jacobs (Ed.), *Planned training on the job* (Vol. 3, Number 4, pp. 425–434). Thousand Oaks, CA: Sage.

Johnston, W. B., & Packer, A. H. (1987). *Workforce 2000: Work and workers for the 21st century*. Indianapolis, IN: Hudson Institute.

Jonassen, D. H. (1982). *The technology of text: Principles for structuring, de-*

signing, and displaying text. Englewood Cliffs, NJ: Educational Technology Publications.

Jonassen, D. H., Hannum, W. H., & Tessmer, M. (1989). *Handbook of task analysis procedures.* New York: Praeger.

Jones, M. J. (2001). Just-in-time training. In R. L. Jacobs (Ed.), *Planned training on the job* (Vol. 3, Number 4, pp. 480–487). Thousand Oaks, CA: Sage.

Jones, M. J., & Jacobs, R. L. (1990). *Implementing synchronous work groups in Fisher-Guide, Columbus: Final report.* Columbus: The Ohio State University.

Jones, M. J., & Jacobs, R. L. (1994). Developing frontline employees: New challenges for achieving organizational effectiveness. In R. Kaufman & T. Sivasailam (Eds.), *Handbook of human performance systems.* San Diego, CA: University Associates.

Kainen, T. L., Begley, T. M., & Maggard, M. J. (1983). On-the-job training and work unit performance. *Training and Development Journal, 37*(4), 84–87.

Kaufman, R. (1998). *Strategic thinking: A guide to identifying and solving problems.* Alexandria, VA: International Society for Performance Improvement and the American Society for Training and Development.

Kaufman, R. (2000). *Mega planning: Practical tools for organizational success.* San Francisco: Sage.

Kaufman, R., & Jones, M. J. (1990). The industrial survival of the nation: Union–management cooperation. *Human Resource Development Quarterly, 1*(1), 87–91.

Kaufman, R., & Zahn, D. (1993). *Quality management plus: The continuous improvement of education.* Newbury Park, CA: Corwin.

Kearney, A. T. (1999). *Enterprise transformation: Mastering the art and science of managing change.* London: Author.

Kim, J. Y., & Lee, C. (2001). Implications of near and far transfer of training on structured on-the-job training. In R. L. Jacobs (Ed.), *Planned training on the job* (Vol. 3, Number 4, pp. 442–451). Thousand Oaks, CA: Sage.

Kirkpatrick, D. L. (1985). Effective supervisory training and development: Part 2. In-house approaches and techniques. *Personnel, 62*(1), 52–56.

Kluch, J., & Whatley, S. (2002). Job consolidation: Structured on-the-job training of non-licensed nuclear operators. In R. L. Jacobs (Ed.), *Implementing on-the-job learning* (pp. 39–50). Alexandra, VA: American Society for Training and Development.

Kondrasuk, J. (1979). The best way to train managers. *Training and Development Journal, 33*(8), 46–48.

Kotter, J., & Heskett, J. (1992). *Corporate culture and performance.* Cambridge, MA: Harvard University Press.

Lave, J., & Wenger, E. (1991). *Situated learning: Legitimate peripheral participation.* Cambridge, MA: Harvard University Press.

Lawson, K. (1997). *Improving on-the-job training and coaching.* Alexandria, VA: American Society for Training and Development.

Leach, J. A. (1991). Characteristics of excellent trainers: A psychological and interpersonal profile. *Performance and Instruction Quarterly, 4*(3), 42–62.

Lee, C., Kim, J., & Jacobs, R. (2002, March). Expanding the Transfer of Training Domain of Structured On-the-Job Training. In A. Oliaga (ed.), *Proceedings of the Annual Conference of the Academy of Human Resource Development.* Bowling Green, OH: Academy of Human Resource Development.

Lee, C., & Yun, Y.-S. (2002). Using the six sigma approach to structured OJT. In R. L. Jacobs (Ed.), *Implementing on-the-job learning* (pp. 51–60). Alexandria, VA: American Society for Training and Development.

Lohman, M. C. (2001). Deductive and inductive on-the-job training strategies. In R. L. Jacobs (Ed.), *Planned training on the job* (Vol. 3, Number 4, pp. 435–441). Thousand Oaks, CA: Sage.

Mafi, S. (2001). Planned on-the-job managerial training. In R. L. Jacobs (Ed.), *Planned training on the job* (Vol. 3, Number 4, pp. 488–495). Thousand Oaks, CA: Sage.

Mager, R. F. (1997). *Preparing instructional objectives,* 3rd ed. Atlanta: Center for Effective Performance.

Mangum, S. (1985). On-the-job vs. classroom training: Some deciding factors. *Training, 22*(2), 75.

Marquardt, M., & Sung, T. (2002). *Building the learning organization.* Palo Alto, CA: Davies-Black.

Marsick, V. J. (1988). Learning in the workplace: The case for reflectivity and critical reflectivity. *Adult Education Quarterly, 38*(4), 187–198.

Marsick, V. J., Cederholm, L., Turner, E., & Pearson, T. (1992, August). Action-reflection learning. *Training and Development,* 63–66.

Marsick, V. J., & Volpe, M. (Eds.). (1999). *Informal learning on the job* (Vol. 1). San Francisco: Berrett-Koehler.

Marsick, V. J., & Watkins, K. (1990). *Informal and incidental learning in the workplace.* London: Routledge.

Martin, V. A. (1991, October). A system for on-the-job training. *Technical and Skills Training, 2*(7), 24–28.

Maxwell, R., & Mosley, T. (2002). Implementing e-learning support and structured communities of practice for effective product development. In R. L. Jacobs (Ed.), *Implementing on-the-job learning* (pp. 61–72). Alexandria, VA: American Society for Training and Development.

McAdam, R., & McKeown, R. (1999). Life after ISO: An analysis of the impact of ISO 9000 and total quality management on small businesses in Northern Ireland. *Total Quality Management, 10*(2), 229–241.

McCord, A. (1987). Job training. In R. L. Craig (Ed.), *Training and development handbook: A guide to human resource development.* New York: McGraw-Hill.

Miller, V. A. (1987). The history of training. In R. L. Craig (Ed.), *Training and development handbook: A guide to human resource development.* New York: McGraw-Hill.

Mirvis, P. H., & Berg, D. N. (1977). *Failures in organizational change.* New York: Wiley.

Molnar, J., Watts, B., & Byrd, J. (2002). Two case studies in training employees with employees. In R. L. Jacobs (Ed.), *Implementing on-the-job learning* (pp. 85–96). Alexandria, VA: American Society for Training and Development.

Osman, A. (2000, January 22). $90 m boost to on-the-job training here. *Singapore Straits Times.*

Osman-Gani, A. M. (2000). Developing expatriates for the Asia–Pacific region: A comparative analysis of multinational enterprise managers from five countries across three continents. *Human Resource Development Quarterly, 11*(3), 213–235.

Osman-Gani, A. M., & Jacobs, R. L. (1996). Differences in perceptions of human resource development across countries: An exploratory study of managers in a multinational enterprise. *Journal of Transnational Management Development, 2*(3), 21–35.

Osman-Gani, A. M., & Zidan, S. S. (2001). Cross-cultural implications of planned training on the job. In R. L. Jacobs (Ed.), *Planned training on the job* (Vol. 3, Number 4, pp. 452–460). Thousand Oaks, CA: Sage.

Pike, B., Solem, L., & Arch, D. (2000). *One-on-one training.* San Francisco: Jossey-Bass.

Pious, J. (1994). *On-the-job training in Singapore: Towards 2000.* Singapore: National Productivity Standards Board.

Powers, B. (1992). *Instructor excellence: Mastering the delivery of training.* San Francisco: Jossey-Bass.

Quazi, H., & Jacobs, R. L. (2002). *Nature and impacts of ISO certification on training and development activities on Singapore organizations.* Paper presented at the Annual Conference of the Academy of Human Resource Development.

Quazi, H., & Padibjo, S. (1998). A journey toward total quality management through ISO 9000 certification: A study of small and medium sized enterprises in Singapore. *International Journal of Quality and Reliability Management, 15*(5), 489–508.

Ramsey, P. (1993). *Successful on-the-job training: Helping others to learn.* Palmerston North, New Zealand: Dunmore.

Robinson, D. G., & Robinson, J. C. (1989). *Training for impact: How to link training to business needs and measure results.* San Francisco: Jossey-Bass.

Robinson, D. G., & Robinson, J. C. (1998). *Moving from training to performance.* San Francisco: Berrett-Koehler.

Rossett, A. (1987). *Training needs assessment.* Englewood Cliffs, NJ: Educational Technology Publications.

Rossett, A., & Gautier-Downes, J. (1991). *A handbook of job aids.* San Diego, CA: Pfeiffer.

Rothwell, W., & Kazanas, H. (1990). Structured on-the-job training (SOJT) as perceived by HRD professionals. *Performance Improvement Quarterly, 3*(3), 12–26.

Rummler, G. A., & Brache, A. P. (1990). *Improving performance: How to manage the white space on the organization chart.* San Francisco: Jossey-Bass.

Russ-Eft, D., & Preskill, H. (2001). *Evaluation in organizations: A systematic approach to enhancing learning, performance, and change.* New York: Perseus.

Schrock, S., & Coscarelli, W. (1989). *Criterion-referenced test development.* Reading, MA: Addison-Wesley.

Semb, G. B., Ellie, J. A., Fitch, M. A., Parchman, S., & Irick, C. (1995). On-the-job training: Prescriptions and practice. *Performance and Instruction, 8*(3), 19–37.

Senge, P. M. (1990). *The fifth discipline: The art and practice of the learning organization.* New York: Doubleday.

Shockley-Zalabak, P., & Buffington Burmester, S. (2001). *The power of networked teams.* New York: Oxford University Press.

Sisson, G. R. (2001). *Hands-on training.* San Francisco: Berrett-Koehler.

Sloman, M. (1989). On-the-job training: A costly poor relation. *Personnel Management, 21*(2), 38–41.

Smith, E. M., Just, D. A., & Prigelmeier, D. R. (2002). Two case studies in a systematic approach to structured on-the-job training for accelerated verifiable results. In R. L. Jacobs (Ed.), *Implementing on-the-job learning* (pp. 111–130). Alexandria, VA: American Society for Training and Development.

Stamps, D. (1998, January). Learning ecologies. *Training.*

Stein, D. (2001). Situated learning and planned training on the job. In R. L. Jacobs (Ed.), *Planned training on the job* (Vol. 3, Number 4, pp. 415–424). Thousand Oaks, CA: Sage.

Stokes, P. M. (1966). *Total job training: A manual for the working manager.* Washington, D.C.: American Management Association.

Stolovitch, H., & Ngoa-Nguele. (2001). Structured on-the-job training in developing nations. In R. L. Jacobs (Ed.), *Planned training on the job* (Vol. 3, Number 4, pp. 461–470). Thousand Oaks, CA: Sage.

Sullivan, R., Brechin, S., & Lacoste, M. (1998). Structured on-the-job training: Innovations in international health training. In W. Rothwell (Ed.), *Linking HRD programs with organizational strategy: Twelve cases from the real world of training* (pp. 155–180). Alexandria, VA: American Society for Training and Development.

Sullivan, R. F., & Miklas, D. C. (1985). On-the-job training that works. *Training and Development Journal, 39*(5), 118–120.

Swanson, R. A. (1994). *Analysis for improving performance: Tools for diagnosing organizations and documenting workplace expertise.* San Francisco: Berrett-Koehler.

Swanson, R. A. (2001). *Assessing the financial benefits of human resource development.* New York: Perseus.

Swanson, R. A., & Law, B. D. (1993). Whole-part-whole learning model. *Performance Improvement Quarterly, 6*(1) 43–53.

Swanson, R. A., & Sawzin, S. A. (1975). *Industrial training research project.* Bowling Green, OH: Bowling Green State University.

Tiemann, P. W., & Markle, S. M. (1983). *Analyzing instructional content: A guide to instruction and evaluation.* Champaign, IL: Stipes.

Tracey, W. R. (1974). *Managing training and development systems.* New York: AMACON.

Utgaard, S. B., & Davis, R. V. (1970). The most frequently used training techniques. *Training and Development Journal, 24*(2), 40–43.

Van Buren, M., & Erskine, W. (2002). *State of the industry: ASTD's annual review of trends in employer-provided training in the United States.* Alexandria, VA: American Society for Training and Development.

Vaught, B. C., Hoy, F., & Buchanan, W. W. (1985). *Employee development programs: An organizational approach.* Westport, CT: Quorum.

Vernon, S. (1999). Learning to be an effective team member. In V. J. Marsick & M. Volpe (Eds.), *Informal learning on the job* (Vol. 3, pp. 33–41). San Francisco: Berrett-Koehler.

Von Bertalanffy, L. (1968). *General system theory: Foundations, development, and applications.* New York: Braziller.

Walter, D. (2002). *Training on the job.* Alexandria, VA: American Society for Training and Development.

Washington, C. (2002). *The relationships among learning transfer climate, transfer self-efficacy, goal commitment, and sales performance in an organization undergoing planned change.* Unpublished Ph.D. dissertation, the Ohio State University, Columbus.

Watkins, K., & Marsick, V. J. (1993). *Sculpting the learning organization: Lessons in the art and science of systemic change.* San Francisco: Jossey-Bass.

Wehrenberg, S. B. (1987). Supervisors as trainers: The long-term gains of OJT. *Personnel Journal, 66*(4), 48–51.

Westgaard, O. (1993). *Good fair tests for use in business and industry.* Amherst, MA: HRD.

Wexley, K. (1988). A tale of two problems: On-the-job training and positive transfer. In R. Schuler, S. Youngblood, & V. Huber (Eds.), *Readings in personnel and human resource management.* St. Paul, MN: West.

Wexley, K. N., & Latham, G. P. (1991). *Developing and training human resources in organizations.* New York: HarperCollins.

Wichman, M. A. (1989). On-the-job training: Formalizing informality or shouldn't supervisors do the training? *Performance and Instruction, 28*(1), 31–32.

Yutaka, K. (1999). *Jinzaikaihaturon (Human Resource Development)* (3rd ed.). Tokyo: Hakutoushobou.

Zemke, R., & Kramlinger, T. (1984). *Figuring things out: A trainer's guide to needs and task analysis.* Reading, MA: Addison-Wesley.

Index

About the Author

Ronald L. Jacobs, Ph.D., is professor of workforce development and education at the Ohio State University. He has written nearly one hundred journal articles and book chapters on a range of human resource development topics, including human competence, employee development, and managing organizational change. In addition, he has edited two books, *Planned Training on the Job* (Sage, 2001) and *Implementing On-the-Job Learning* (ASTD, 2002). He is a frequent speaker at professional meetings and conferences. Ron is particularly known for his research and development work on *structured on-the-job training,* a term that he first introduced to the human resource development literature in 1987. Much of his research has been on determining the financial benefits of structured OJT, information that is critical for making more informed training investment decisions.

Ron has consulted extensively in both manufacturing and service organizations, having worked for numerous large organizations such as American Electric Power, General Motors, KLM Airlines, Abbott Laboratories, Seagate, and Rohm and Haas. He has presented and consulted internationally in Taiwan, South Korea, Egypt, Brazil, Mexico, Germany, Italy, Slovenia, Singapore, the Netherlands, and Kuwait, among other countries. Ron has taught at Utrecht University, the Netherlands, and held a distinguished visiting professorship at the School of Business, Nanyang Technological University, Singapore.

In 1994, Ron received the instructional technology re-search award from the American Society for Training and Development, and in 1995, he was recognized for his schol-arly contributions to the HRD field by the Academy of Human Resource Development. Ron has served as the editor of the *Human Resource Development Quarterly*, the major scholarly journal of the human resource development field. His interests include sailing, golf, and home restoration.

Spread the word!

Berrett-Koehler books and audios are available at quantity discounts for orders of 10 or more copies.

Structured On-the-Job Training
Unleashing Employee Expertise in the Workplace
Ronald L. Jacobs

Hardcover, 220 pages
ISBN 1-88105-220-6
Item #52206-415 $29.05

To find out about discounts on orders of 10 or more copies for individuals, corporations, institutions, and organizations, please call us toll-free at (800) 929-2929.

To find out about our discount programs for resellers, please contact our Special Sales department at (415) 288-0260; Fax: (415) 362-2512. Or email us at bkpub@bkpub.com.

Berrett-Koehler Publishers
PO Box 565, Williston, VT 05495-9900
Call toll-free! **800-929-2929** 7 am-9 pm Eastern Standard Time
Or fax your order to 802-864-7627
For fastest service order online: **www.bkconnection.com**